Mastering Personal Finance for Teens

7 EASY STEPS TO SAVING, BUDGETING, AND INVESTING TO GAIN FINANCIAL INDEPENDENCE FOR A DEBT-FREE TOMORROW

E.J. GOLDWYN

R.O. Publishing Ventures

CONTENTS

INTRODUCTION

Did you know that nearly 60% of young adults wish they had received more financial education while growing up? Let's face it, the financial decisions you make today can shape your tomorrow, and yet, many teens find themselves trying to make important money choices without a clue. Picture Jake, a high school junior, staring at his first paycheck, puzzled about taxes, savings, or whether he could afford that new video game console. Like Jake, you might be facing or soon facing similar situations. This book is your guide to navigating these murky waters with confidence.

"Mastering Personal Finance for Teens: 7 Easy Steps to Saving, Budgeting, and Investing To Gain Financial Independence for a Debt-Free Tomorrow" is crafted with a clear mission—to empower you with the financial knowledge and skills that pave the way for real independence and success. This isn't just another adult's guide awkwardly repurposed for a younger audience; it's written for you, about you, and speaking directly to your experiences and challenges.

Let's break it down together through seven straightforward steps: understanding your money mindset, setting up and sticking to a budget, smart saving strategies, the basics of investing, handling taxes, making sense of credit cards, and planning for future goals like college or your first car. Each step is designed to build on the previous one, creating a solid foundation of financial know-how.

Why start now? Research shows that teens who grasp the fundamentals of budgeting and saving are better equipped to handle their money responsibly as adults. You have the incredible opportunity to get ahead of the curve, avoiding common pitfalls that snag many young adults.

As the author of this book, I bring my journey of financial discoveries, mistakes, and lessons learned directly to you. I've navigated the highs and lows of personal finance, from scrambling to pay for unexpected college expenses to learning the power of a well-planned investment. Sharing these experiences is not just my job but my passion, especially when it helps someone like you take control of their financial destiny.

This book isn't just about reading; it's about doing. You'll find practical tools and even interactive quizzes to keep you engaged and help apply what you learn directly to your life. Each chapter is a stepping stone toward not only understanding money but mastering it.

Imagine a future where you're not just debt-free but are fully in charge of your financial situation, capable of making informed decisions that lead to a secure and prosperous life. That future is not only possible, it's within reach, and it starts with the steps laid out in this book.

So, are you ready to take charge of your financial future? Let's get started on this journey together, and turn those dreams into achievable goals.

CHAPTER 1

FOUNDATIONS OF FINANCIAL LITERACY

Hey! Ready to become a financial whiz? This isn't your average snooze-fest finance class. Think of this as your personal finance cheat sheet, where you'll unlock the secrets to making your money work for you, starting with the very basics. We're talking about the fundamentals here, the groundwork of all money management. And guess what? Understanding this stuff now puts you way ahead of the curve, and let's be honest, it's kind of empowering to know you're getting smarter about your cash.

Before you can run, you've got to walk, right? In this chapter, we're going to decode some of the most thrown-around financial terms that often leave people scratching their heads. Why? Because knowing these terms is like holding the keys to a secret club. The more you know, the better you navigate through the world of money without getting tripped up. So let's get into it!

1.1 Decoding Financial Jargon: Terms Every Teen Should Know

Common Financial Terms

First up, let's talk APR. Ever heard of it? APR stands for Annual Percentage Rate. It's basically the extra amount you'll pay on what you borrow or earn extra on what you save, spread out over a year. Think of it as the cost of borrowing money or the bonus for saving it. For instance, if you get a credit card with an APR of 20%, and you carry a balance of $100 on your card, you'll owe about $20 in interest over the year. On the flip side, if a savings account offered you an APR of 2%, and you deposit $100, congrats, you just made an extra two bucks by the end of the year.

Next, we have compound interest, a term that might sound like rocket science but stick with me—it's pretty cool. Compound interest is when you earn interest not just on your initial amount of money but also on the interest it accumulates over time. So, if you save $100 and your bank offers 5% interest annually, you don't just keep earning $5 every year. Instead, that interest also starts earning interest. Over many years, this can turn your modest savings into a hefty sum without you having to lift a finger!

Lastly, let's unravel liquidity. This isn't about how much water you drink. In finance, liquidity refers to how quickly you can turn an asset (like stocks, bonds, or even a fancy stamp collection) into cash without losing value. Cash itself is super liquid because, well, it's already cash. But something like a house? Not so much, since it can take months to sell.

Interactive Glossary

To keep all this jargon straight, why not start a glossary? I've started one for you in the back of this book but you can also jot down these terms and their definitions in a notebook or make a digital doc on your phone. Every time you come across a new financial term, add it to the list! Not only does this build your financial vocabulary, but it also makes you the go-to person among your friends for money advice (talk about a win).

Real-Life Application

Try this out: next time you're about to stash your cash in a savings account or you're looking at different credit card offers, pause and consider the terms we just talked about. Which account offers the best APR? How does the compound interest on different accounts compare? This isn't just about making smarter choices; it's about building habits that will pay off big time in the future.

Got all that? Great! You're now officially on your way to becoming a finance pro. Keep these terms in mind as you move forward, and remember, every bit of knowledge is a step towards making more informed and confident financial decisions. Keep adding to that glossary, and watch how these concepts start popping up in your everyday money moves!

1.2 How Money Works: Understanding Currency, Banking, and Interest Rates

Let's take a step back in time, shall we? Imagine a world where if you wanted to buy some bread and cheese, you'd have to trade maybe a goat and a basket of wheat. Sounds bizarre, right? Well, that was the reality in the barter system era, where goods were exchanged for other goods without any money changing hands. Fast forward to today, and money, in all its glory—from coins and bills to digital currency—makes our modern economy tick. It's fascinating to see how money has evolved from physical bartering to digital

transactions where you can pay with just a tap on your phone. This evolution has made transactions smoother and lets us focus more on what we're buying rather than how to carry dozens of eggs to the market!

Now, let's talk banks. Banks are like the big leagues for your money. They keep it safe, yes, but they also do a lot more. Banks offer various services like savings accounts to stash your cash, loans for when you need more cash, and even things like mortgages, which you might have to think about later in life when you're considering buying a house. For now, you might be more interested in how banks can help you with a student loan or your first checking account. Here's the thing: banks can actually help you grow your money. When you keep your money in a savings account, the bank pays you interest, which means your money increases over time, without you having to do any extra work.

Speaking of interest, let's break down interest rates because they're pretty much everywhere. An interest rate is basically a percentage that tells you how much extra money you will earn or owe. When you save money in a bank, the interest rate determines how much extra money the bank will pay you for letting them use your money. On the flip side, if you borrow money, the interest rate tells you how much extra you'll need to pay back on top of what you borrowed. So, if you're choosing a savings account or considering a loan, comparing interest rates is a must to make sure you're getting the best deal. It's like shopping for a new phone—you want the best features for the best price, right?

Now, for some down-to-earth advice on dealing with banks. When choosing a bank, think about what's important to you. Do you want a bank with lots of ATMs nearby? Or maybe one that has a great mobile app? Once you've chosen a bank and start using your account, keeping an eye on your bank statement is crucial. A bank statement is a summary of all the transactions in your account. It tells you how much money went in or out, and when. It's like a financial diary that helps you track where your money is going, which is super helpful for managing your finances and spotting any errors or suspicious activities.

Understanding how money works, the role of banks, and the impact of interest rates on personal finances isn't just useful, it's essential for making informed financial decisions. Whether you're saving up for something big, like college, or just managing your weekly allowance, getting to grips with these basics will set you up for financial success. And remember, every pro was once a beginner, so you're on the right track. Keep building your financial knowledge, and soon, managing money will feel as easy as spending it—maybe even easier!

1.3 Setting Your Financial Goals: Short, Medium, and Long Term

Let's talk about something super exciting—setting financial goals. Now, you might be thinking, "Why is setting goals exciting?" Well, it's like plotting your personal roadmap to buying that gadget you've been eyeing, or even bigger stuff like owning a car or not drowning in student loans. Financial goals aren't just about saving money; they're about giving you the power to make your dreams a reality. Think about it: with no goals, managing money can feel like wandering through a huge city without a map, just hoping you'll stumble upon the places you want to visit. But with goals? You've got a GPS that guides every financial decision you make, big or small.

Let's break it down with some examples. Short-term goals are like the snacks of financial planning—they keep you fueled and are relatively quick to achieve. Say you want to go to a concert next month. You figure out the ticket cost, maybe add a bit extra for merch, and start setting aside a bit of cash from your weekly allowance or that tutoring gig. Medium-term goals, however, are more like preparing a solid meal. These goals require a bit more planning and saving. Think about buying a used car. It's not something you can achieve in a month, right? You'll need to research costs, maybe compare models and prices, and start saving a portion of money from a summer job or ongoing side hustles.

Then we have the big kahunas—long-term goals. These are like planning a feast that takes more time and ingredients. A common long-term goal is saving for college. This isn't just about tuition; it's also about books, living expenses, and maybe some funds for social activities. Starting to save for this as early as possible can make a huge difference, reducing the amount you might need to borrow when the college years kick off.

Now, how do you set these goals so that they're not just wishes? Enter SMART goals—Specific, Measurable, Achievable, Relevant, Time-bound. Let's say your goal is to buy a car. A SMART goal would look something like this: "I will save $3,000 for a used car by saving $250 every month from my part-time job for the next 12 months." This goal isn't just a vague "I want a car"; it's a clear plan with steps defined to make it achievable.

But how do you keep track of your progress? Visual goal tracking can be a game-changer here. You could use a simple chart in your room where you fill in a bar every time you save money toward your goals. Apps can also be super helpful. Many apps not only track your savings but also motivate you with reminders and visual progress bars. Seeing a visual representation of your savings growing can boost your motivation to keep pushing towards your goal, turning the abstract concept of saving into something tangible and exciting.

Remember, setting financial goals isn't just about securing your future; it's about making your money meaningful in the present. It turns abstract numbers into real-world fun and fulfillment. Whether it's a concert, a car, or college, each goal you set and reach brings you one step closer to financial savvy and independence. So, why wait? Start plotting your course now, and watch how your financial goals turn into financial successes, one smart, achievable step at a time.

1.4 The Magic of Budgeting: Creating Your First Budget

Let's talk about budgeting. Yes, the word might sound about as fun as watching paint dry, but trust me, it's not just a bunch of numbers on a spreadsheet. Think of it as your financial game plan for scoring goals like that epic summer road trip or the latest smartphone. A budget is essentially a blueprint for your money, ensuring you know where every dollar is going (so it doesn't just wander off on its own).

So, why is budgeting crucial? Imagine planning to build a dream gaming setup. You wouldn't just go out and start buying random parts without knowing what you need and how much you can spend, right? Budgeting works the same way. It keeps you from spending more than you earn, so you don't end up in a financial mess, staring at a bank statement and wondering where all your money went. Plus, it's pretty satisfying to see your savings grow because you're sticking to a plan.

Let's break down how to create a simple, no-fuss budget. First, grab a piece of paper, or better yet, open a new spreadsheet on your computer or smartphone. Start by listing all your sources of income. This could be your allowance, money from a part-time job, or that cash you get from babysitting every weekend. Add it all up. This total is what you have to work with every month—your total income.

Next, track where that money is going. Write down your regular expenses like phone bills, transportation costs, and yes, even that coffee you grab on the way to school. Don't forget to include occasional expenses like birthday gifts or emergency pizza funds. Subtract your total expenses from your total income, and boom—you've got a clear picture of how much you can save or how much more you need to cut back.

Now, here's where it gets tech-savvy. There are tons of apps and online tools that can make budgeting as easy as snapping a selfie. Apps like Mint or You Need a Budget (YNAB) link directly to your bank account and categorize your spending for you. They can even send you alerts when you're spending too fast or congratulate you when you stick to your budget. If apps aren't your thing, spreadsheets are just as effective. Google Sheets or Microsoft Excel have built-in templates for budgeting that you can customize as much as you like.

But hey, let's be real—budgeting isn't always a walk in the park. One of the biggest challenges you might face is sticking to your budget when it feels like everyone around you is splurging. It's tough, but remember, every time you choose to stick to your budget, you're building up your financial strength, which is way cooler than impulse buys.

Another common hiccup is underestimating expenses. Maybe you forgot to account for that monthly music streaming subscription, or maybe you didn't realize how much you were actually spending on snacks after school. It happens to the best of us. The key is to review your budget regularly and adjust it as needed. This doesn't mean you failed; it means you're fine-tuning your budgeting skills. It's all part of the process.

Budgeting is like learning a new song on the guitar or mastering a new video game level—it gets easier with practice. The more you do it, the better you get, and soon, it'll feel like second nature. By taking control of your money now, you're setting yourself up for a future where financial worries don't hold you back from achieving your dreams. So, why not start today and see where a solid budget can take you? After all, those financial goals aren't going to achieve themselves!

1.5 Essentials of Saving: Why, How, and Where to Save

Ah, saving money, the unsung hero of financial wellness. We often hear adults drone on about saving for the future, and while it might sound like a lecture, they're not entirely off base. Think about it: money in the bank isn't just about stashing cash for the distant future. It's also about having the freedom to jump on unexpected opportunities or cover those "oh no" moments when life throws a curveball. Let's say you suddenly get the chance to go on a dream road trip with friends or, less fun, your smartphone gives out. Having some money saved up means you're ready to seize adventures or tackle emergencies without breaking a sweat (or the bank).

Now, where to stash that cash? There are more options than just hiding it under your mattress, and each comes with its own set of pros and cons. First up, high-interest savings accounts. These are like the reliable sedans of the saving world: not super flashy but dependable and a good place to start. They offer higher interest rates than regular savings accounts, which means your money grows faster without you doing anything. It's like making money in your sleep, which is pretty awesome.

Then there are Certificates of Deposit (CDs), the time capsules of finance. You put in a fixed amount of money for a fixed period, and boom, you earn interest at a higher rate than savings accounts. The catch? You can't touch the money for a while without facing a penalty. It's perfect if you have a future expense and want to remove the temptation to spend prematurely.

Money market accounts? They're the SUVs: stronger and more robust. These usually offer higher interest rates than both regular savings and high-interest accounts, plus you can often write checks or use debit cards directly linked to these accounts. This flexibility is great, but they often require a higher minimum balance, so it's something to consider once you've got a good saving buffer.

So, how do you make saving a no-brainer habit? Start by setting up automatic transfers from your checking account to your savings account. It's like setting a fitness goal; automate it, and you won't have to pump yourself up to make a transfer every month—it just happens. Also, think about saving any unexpected cash—birthday money, a bonus from a part-time job, or even cash from selling old video games online. Instead of blowing it on impulse buys, redirect some (or all) of that windfall into your savings.

Before you know it, you'll have a nice cushion to support your goals or cover emergencies.

Banks, knowing that everyone loves a good perk, often dangle carrots to attract young savers like you. No-fee accounts are a common sweetener, meaning you won't get dinged with annoying charges just for keeping your money in the bank. Some even offer signup bonuses or extra interest rates if you open an account and meet certain conditions, like maintaining a minimum balance or setting up direct deposits. These incentives can add up and boost your savings without any extra effort on your part.

Remember, saving is more than a financial strategy; it's about building the freedom to pursue opportunities and handle challenges without stress. Whether you're saving for a concert ticket, a college textbook, or just a rainy day, each dollar you tuck away is setting you up for financial success and security. So why not start today? Your future self will thank you—and maybe even treat you to something nice with all the interest you've earned. And hey, getting into the habit of saving now means you'll be way ahead of the game when bigger financial goals come into play. So, let's keep this savings party going, shall we? After all, every dollar saved today is a step toward a more financially secure tomorrow.

1.6 Smart Spending: Learning to Prioritize Wants vs. Needs

Alright, let's get real about spending. You've probably heard the old "needs vs. wants" lecture a few times, right? Maybe from parents right before they say no to that new pair of sneakers you've been eyeing. But understanding this concept can seriously level up your financial game. Needs are things you must have to live and function—think food, shelter, basic clothing, and transportation. Wants, on the other hand, are things that are nice to have but you won't, you know, perish without them. That latest gaming console? Definitely a want. The latest iPhone when your current one works just fine? Also a want.

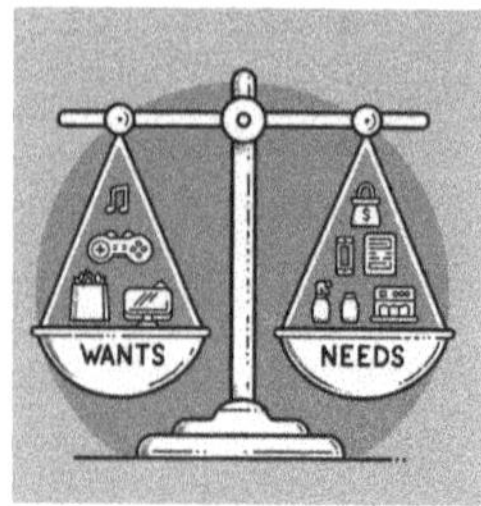

But hey, life isn't just about surviving; it's about enjoying things too. The trick is figuring out how to balance your needs and wants without ending up broke. That's where prioritization techniques come into play, like the famous "50/30/20 rule." It's pretty straightforward: 50% of your budget goes to needs, 30% to wants, and 20% to savings or debt repayment. It's a cool rule because it keeps you in check, ensuring you're covering essentials while still leaving room for fun and future goals. This method isn't just about restricting; it's about empowering you to make smart choices with your money.

Now, let's talk about the elephant in the store: impulse buying. Ever walked into a store (or fine, clicked on a website) planning to buy one thing, and somehow left with five? That's impulse buying and it's driven by psychological triggers like emotions (ever heard of retail therapy?) or even marketing tactics (those 'limited time offers' can be tempting). To combat this wallet-draining habit, try setting a waiting period rule. If you see something you think you must have, wait 48 hours before buying it. Often, the urge to buy will pass, and you'll save money and regret. Another tip? Make a shopping list before you go to the store and stick to it, no matter how tempting those aisle-end specials might be.

Conscious consumption is another superhero skill that can save your bank account. It means thinking critically about each purchase: How much will you use it? Do you already own something that does the same thing? Could that money be better spent or saved for a bigger goal? For example, let's say you're considering buying a designer jacket. It looks cool, sure, but it's pricey. Thinking it through, you might realize that a more affordable jacket would keep you just as warm and leave you with cash left over for other things, like hanging out with friends or adding to your savings. Being a conscious consumer doesn't mean you never get to splurge, but it does mean making those splurges count.

So, as you navigate the mall or browse online stores, keep these ideas in mind. Balancing needs and wants, setting spending boundaries, and thinking critically about purchases can transform the way you handle money. It's not just about saving dollars; it's about making smarter decisions that align with your goals and values. Remember, every smart financial decision you make today is a step toward a more secure and enjoyable tomorrow. So, next time you reach for your wallet, take a moment to think: is this a need, a want, or maybe something that can wait? Your bank account (and future self) will thank you.

Financial Savvy Quiz

To check your understanding of financial terms and concepts, take this quick quiz! Jot down your answers and find out how financially literate you are:

1. Do you know what APR stands for and how it affects borrowing and saving money?   Yes / No

2. Have you started a personal glossary of financial terms to help you understand and remember them?   Yes / No

3. When choosing a savings account, do you consider the impact of compound interest on your savings?   Yes / No

4. Do you understand the importance of liquidity and how quickly you can convert assets into cash without losing value?   Yes / No

Count your 'Yes' answers:

- **4** means you're a financial whiz!

- **3-2** suggests you're well on your way but could use a bit more fine-tuning.

- **1 or below**? Let's boost your financial knowledge to ensure you're ready for financial success!

CHAPTER 2

MASTERING MONEY MANAGEMENT

Ever felt like your money just magically disappears? One minute you're feeling like a millionaire after getting your allowance or paycheck, and the next, you're digging through the couch cushions looking for spare change. If this sounds familiar, then buckle up! It's time to take a deep dive into managing your money like a pro. And no, you won't need a fancy finance degree to do it. All you need is a little know-how, some discipline, and maybe a few envelopes. Yes, envelopes! Let's kick things off with a classic but super effective method to keep your spending in check—the Envelope System.

2.1 The Envelope System: A Visual Method for Managing Cash

Introduction to the Envelope System

Imagine you're the director of your own movie, and this movie is about the epic adventure of your cash. The envelope system is your script. Here's the gist: instead of letting your cash roam wild and free, you assign it specific roles (or "parts" in our movie analogy). Each role is a spending category like food, entertainment, or savings, and each category gets its own envelope filled with the cash you're allowing it to spend for the month. It's like giving each dollar a job application, interviewing it, and then hiring it to do a specific task.

Setting Up the System

Setting up your envelope system is easier than assembling IKEA furniture, I promise. First, write down your regular spending categories. These might include groceries, gas, going out, and whatever else you regularly spend money on. Now, decide how much money you want to spend in each category for the month. This part requires a bit of math and some tough decision-making. It's about figuring out your priorities—maybe you decide to cut back on eating out so you can save up for a concert ticket.

Once you've got your categories and cash limits set, label your envelopes accordingly. Each payday, withdraw the budgeted amounts in cash and distribute the money among the envelopes. If you get $50 for entertainment for the month, that's all you put in the 'Entertainment' envelope. When the envelope is empty, that's your cue: no more spending in that category until next month! It's like a traffic light system that tells you when to go and when to stop.

Benefits of Visual and Physical Budgeting

This method might sound a bit old-school, but there's magic in its simplicity. Physically dividing your money into envelopes makes your budget super tangible. You're not just swiping cards and forgetting about it; you actually see your money, feel it, and watch it go places (or not go places if you're saving up). This can be a real eye-opener and a game-changer in how you perceive and spend your money. It turns abstract numbers into real, tangible things. Running low on your 'Fun Money' envelope? You might think twice about buying that extra frappuccino.

Transitioning to Digital Envelopes

Now, if carrying around a bunch of envelopes isn't your style or you're more of a digital native, there's a high-tech version just for you. Several apps mimic the envelope system without the paper cuts. Apps like Goodbudget or Mvelopes let you create digital envelopes on your smartphone. You allocate your money into different categories just like the physical method, but it's all tracked on your phone, so you always know how much you have left to spend in each category. Plus, it's less risky than carrying around your entire cash allowance. These apps can sync across devices, so you can manage your budget on the go and even share it with family members if you're working on a joint budget. It's like having a financial advisor in your pocket, minus the advisor fees.

The envelope system, whether physical or digital, could seriously level up your money management game. It's straightforward, effective, and it gives you a clear picture of where your money is going each month. Plus, it's pretty satisfying to see your savings envelope get thicker as you get closer to your goals. So why not give it a try? Who knows, you might just get a kick out of budgeting after all.

2.2 Digital Tools for Budgeting: Apps and Platforms for Teens

In this era of smartphones and instant notifications, managing your money has never been easier, or to be frank, cooler. Gone are the days of balancing checkbooks manually or tracking expenses on clunky spreadsheets. Today, a slew of user-friendly budgeting apps are designed just for teens and young adults who want to take control of their cash without the hassle. These apps aren't just about tracking what you spend—they can help you set goals, save smart, and even get reminders about bills that are due so you don't end up paying late fees (because who wants to waste money on that?).

First off, let's talk about some standout apps that are perfect for teens dipping their toes into the financial management world. Take 'Mint', for example, it's like the Swiss Army knife of budgeting tools. It links to your bank accounts, tracks your spending, and categorizes everything automatically. It even gives you a nudge when you're spending too much on pizza or those late-night online shopping sprees. Then there's 'YNAB' (You Need A Budget), which is great if you're trying to really get a handle on your future spending. It encourages you to plan for every dollar so you can reach your financial goals faster, whether that's saving up for a new laptop or managing money for college.

Choosing the right app can feel a bit like dating—what works for one person might not be the right match for another. So, when you're app hunting, think about what you really need. Are you looking for something that will just track your spending, or do you need something that will help you plan your entire financial future? Also, check out the security features—after all, you'll be linking this app to your bank accounts. Look for apps that offer encryption and are backed by reputable companies. Ease of use is another big one. If you find yourself scratching your head two minutes into using the app, it's probably not the one for you. The best apps have clean, intuitive interfaces that make managing your money feel almost fun.

Now, on to linking these apps with your bank accounts. This might sound a bit scary, but it's actually safe as long as you're using a reputable app. These apps use some pretty heavy-duty encryption to protect your data. Linking your accounts can make budgeting a lot easier because transactions are automatically updated and categorized. This means you can see exactly where your money is going in real time, which is pretty handy. Just make sure you've got a strong password set up and that you're comfortable with the app's privacy policy before you dive in.

Speaking of privacy and security, let's hammer this home: guarding your financial information is super important. Always use a strong, unique password for your financial apps—not your birthday or your pet's name. Consider using a password manager to keep track of your passwords if you're juggling a few. Enable two-factor authentication if the app offers it; this adds an extra layer of security by requiring not just your password but also a code sent to your phone to access your account. And always, always log out of your apps when you're done, especially if you're using a shared or public device. You wouldn't leave your wallet lying around at a cafe, right? Treat your financial apps with the same care.

These digital tools are more than just apps; they're your partners in making sure you're making the most out of every dollar you earn or receive. By setting up the right app, linking it securely with your bank accounts, and following smart security practices, you're setting yourself up not just for better budgeting but for a financially savvy future. So why not start exploring these digital tools today? After all, your financial independence isn't just a dream—it's just an app away.

2.3 Overcoming Common Financial Challenges: Tips for Staying on Budget

Let's face it, sticking to a budget can sometimes feel like trying to stick to a diet during the holiday season—pretty darn tough. Especially when you're a teen, and it seems like every weekend there's something going on that just screams for you to spend money. Whether it's catching a movie with friends, grabbing a bite, or those unexpected "must-have" purchases, staying on budget can sometimes seem like an epic quest from a high fantasy novel. But fear not! You're not alone in this adventure, and believe it or not, it's totally possible to manage your money without missing out on the fun.

First up, let's talk about one of the biggies: social spending. It's those times when you're out with friends, and everyone decides to get the deluxe meal, or when you're at a concert, and the merch stand is calling your name. Here's a pro tip: plan ahead. If you know you've got a social event coming up, think about how much it might cost and make sure you set aside some cash for it in your budget. It's like saving up your appetite before a big feast—you know you're going to indulge a little, so you prepare accordingly.

Then there's the bane of every budgeter's existence: unexpected expenses. These are the curveballs life throws at you, like your phone screen deciding to impersonate a spiderweb or your favorite pair of jeans developing an impromptu hole. This is where having an emergency fund becomes a game-changer. Try to funnel a small part of your budget into an emergency fund each month. Even if it's just a few dollars, it adds up over time and can be a lifesaver  when you need cash fast and don't want to derail your financial goals.

Now, what happens when your budget needs a little tweak? Maybe you got a new part-time job, or your expenses have changed because school started, or ended. That's totally normal, and your budget should be flexible enough to keep up with your life's ups and downs. Every month, take a moment to look over your budget and see if it still makes sense. Maybe you need to adjust how much you're spending on groceries or transport. Or maybe you can finally increase the amount you throw into your savings each month. Think of your budget like a playlist—sometimes you've got to swap out a few songs to keep it fresh and exciting.

But here's the real secret sauce to sticking with a budget: motivation. Sometimes, you just need a little pep talk to remind yourself why you're doing all this in the first place. Set small, achievable financial goals that get you pumped. Maybe it's saving up for a new skateboard, or a concert ticket, or just having a cushion of cash for peace of mind. Whatever it is, let that goal be your north star, guiding your spending decisions and keeping you focused. And don't forget to celebrate when you hit those goals! Rewarding yourself for a job well done (without breaking the bank, of course) can boost your morale and keep your financial spirits high.

So, there you have it. Sticking to a budget might have its challenges, but with a bit of planning, a dash of flexibility, and a sprinkle of motivation, you can manage your money like a pro. Remember, every smart financial decision you make not only brings you closer to your short-term goals but also lays the groundwork for your long-term financial success. So keep at it, adjust as needed, and watch your financial confidence grow—one budgeted dollar at a time.

2.4 Strategies for Growing Your Savings: Beyond the Piggy Bank

Advanced Saving Strategies

So, you've been saving money in your piggy bank since you could barely count—kudos! But let's kick things up a notch. Ever heard of compound interest? Imagine it as your money making its own money, which then goes on to make more money—kind of like a family tree but with cash. Here's how it works: you put some money in a savings account, and it earns interest. Next year, you earn interest on both your initial money *and* the interest from last year. Over time, this snowballs, and before you know it, you've got a heap more than you started with.

Understanding compound interest can seriously amp up your saving game. It's like being in a video game where you're not just collecting coins; you're earning points on those coins too! Banks and credit unions offer various savings accounts that capitalize on this concept, so by depositing your money and letting it sit, you're actually making more money without lifting a finger. Magic, right? Well, no, it's just smart finance—using the power of time and a little patience.

Setting Up Dedicated Savings Accounts

Your next step? Get yourself a dedicated savings account. Think of it like having different baskets for different types of eggs. You might want an account for immediate fun money, another for college savings, and maybe one for emergency cash. High-yield savings accounts are the golden geese here because they offer higher interest rates than standard accounts, meaning your money grows faster.

Opening these accounts is usually a breeze. Most banks and credit unions offer online applications where you just fill out some details, and boom, you're ready to start saving. The key is to look for accounts with no month-ly fees and high interest rates. And don't be shy to shop around or ask questions. It's your money, after all, so you want to make sure it's in the right place, growing at the best rate possible.

Using Technology to Boost Savings

Let's 'tech' things up a notch. Did you know there are apps designed to boost your savings without you even noticing? These apps round up your purchases to the nearest dollar and stash the difference in a savings account. For example, if you buy a burger for $4.20, the app rounds it up to $5 and puts $0.80 into savings. It might not seem like much, but over time, and with enough purchases, this can add up to a significant amount. It's like turning your digital spare change into a growing money plant.

These apps are especially handy because they link directly to your bank account and do all the heavy lifting for you, making saving as passive and painless as possible. Just make sure to check the app settings so you can customize how and when you save, keeping control over your cash flow.

Creative Saving Challenges

Finally, let's make saving a bit more fun with some creative challenges. Ever tried a no-spend week? That's right, you challenge yourself to spend zero on non-essential items for a whole week. All the money you would have spent? Into savings it goes. Or how about the 52-week money challenge? You start by saving $1 in the first week, $2 in the second, and so on, right up to $52 in the last week of the year. By the end, you'll have tucked away a tidy sum of $1,378!

You can even turn saving into a competition with friends or family to see who can save the most money in a month, using an app to track everyone's progress. Throw in a fun reward for the winner (using a small portion of the saved money, of course), and you've got yourself a savings race. These challenges not only make saving money a bit more exciting but also build good habits that can last a lifetime.

By understanding and utilizing strategies like compound interest, setting up dedicated savings accounts, leveraging technology, and engaging in fun saving challenges, you're on your way to making your savings account something worth bragging about. Remember, every little bit adds up, and the sooner you start, the better off you'll be. So, why not give these strategies a try and watch your savings grow? After all, the only thing better than having money is having more of it!

2.5 The Psychology of Spending: Understanding Impulse Purchases

Ever wandered into a store—or let's be real, scrolled through an online shop—and ended up buying something totally unplanned? Maybe it was that cool hoodie that popped up in an ad, or those sneakers you saw someone wearing in a TikTok video. Suddenly, you're typing in your credit card info, thinking, "I've gotta have it!" Welcome to the world of impulse buying, where emotions rule and wallets sometimes suffer. But why do we give in to these sudden urges to spend? Turns out, it's not just about the stuff we buy—it's about how buying makes us feel.

Understanding emotional spending starts with recognizing the triggers. Stress, for instance, is a big one. Ever had a rough day at school and found yourself munching on a pricey pastry at the nearest café, or buying a game to blow off some steam? That's emotional spending. Excitement can do it too. Maybe you just aced a test, and that 'treat yourself' vibe kicks in, nudging you toward buying something as a reward. Peer pressure also plays a role. Seeing friends or influencers flaunting the latest gadgets or fashion can stir up a fear of missing out (FOMO), pushing you to buy just to keep up.

Now, how do you get a grip on these impulses? One super effective technique is the 24-hour rule, especially for bigger, non-essential purchases. Here's the deal: when you feel that rush to buy something, pause and give yourself 24 hours to think it over. It's not about saying no—it's about saying "let me sleep on it." You'd be surprised how often something that felt like a must-have turns into a "meh" after a good night's sleep. This pause helps you step back from the emotional edge and decide if it's really worth your hard-earned cash.

Reflective practices can also help you master your spending impulses. Try keeping a spending diary for a month. Jot down what you bought, how much it cost, and what you were feeling at the time. Were you bored? Happy? Stressed? After a few weeks, patterns will start to emerge. You might notice that stress often leads you to the nearest online store, or that hanging out with certain friends always ends up in a shopping spree. Seeing these patterns can be a real eye-opener, helping you understand and eventually reshape your spending habits.

Building mindful spending habits is key to aligning your spending with your long-term financial goals. Start by setting clear goals—like saving for college, a new laptop, or a car. Then, before each purchase, ask yourself: "Does this help me reach my goals?" If it doesn't, consider putting it back on the shelf. Another tip? Set a budget for fun or discretionary spending. This gives you a safe space to enjoy shopping without derailing your financial goals. Think of it as your financial sandbox—inside, you can play around, but outside of it, it's all about sticking to your goals.

Remember, understanding the psychology behind your spending isn't about cutting all the fun out of your life. It's about making smarter choices that help you take control of your cash and your future. Whether it's resisting the pull of impulse buys, reflecting on your spending triggers, or making mindful choices that align with your dreams, every step you take is building a stronger, savvier financial you. So next time you feel the itch to splurge on something on a whim, take a moment to check in with yourself. Your wallet—and your future self—will thank you.

2.6 Financial Responsibility: Handling Money with Care

Navigating the world of personal finance isn't just about knowing how to save or spend; it's also about cultivating a sense of responsibility towards yourself and the wider community. Think of it as the superhero creed but for handling money: with great power (or cash) comes great responsibility. So, how do you wield this power wisely? Well, it starts with a commitment to self-discipline. Managing your personal finances carefully ensures you're not just living for today but are also prepping for tomorrow. This means being punctual with the management of your earnings and allowances. If you've earmarked funds for specific purposes—like saving for that new video game or paying off a small debt—stick to it. It's like making a promise to yourself and keeping it, which, let's be honest, feels pretty good.

Now, while being responsible for your own finances is cool and all, there's also a civic side to this coin—understanding taxes. Yeah, taxes might sound about as exciting as watching paint dry, but they're a crucial part of financial literacy. If you're working part-time or pulling in cash from a side hustle, getting a handle on how taxes work will save you from a lot of headaches down the road. For example, knowing how to file a simple tax return and understanding what deductions you're eligible for can not only keep you compliant with the law but might also save you some money. Plus, it's empowering to know where your money is going, like seeing how it's used for public services and infrastructure. Being tax-savvy means you're not just earning money; you're also contributing responsibly to the big societal pot.

Ethical spending is another facet of financial responsibility. This means thinking about the impact your money has when you spend it. Supporting businesses that align with your values—be it environmental sustainability, fair labor practices, or local community support—can make a significant difference. Every dollar you spend is like casting a vote for the kind of world you want to live in. So, next time you're about to purchase something, take a moment to consider who and what you're supporting. It might lead you to discover some cool local artists or eco-friendly businesses that are working to make a difference, not just a profit.

Lastly, let's talk about the long game: long-term financial planning. It's never too early to start thinking about the future, and a big part of that is making sure you're prepared for any financial surprises life might throw your way. This includes understanding the basics of insurance—whether it's health, car, or renter's insurance. Knowing you're covered in case of an accident or emergency can provide peace of mind and financial stability. Also, planning for long-term financial goals like buying a house or funding your retirement might seem light years away, but laying the groundwork now by understanding these concepts will put you miles ahead later.

While the immediate benefits of financial responsibility like staying debt-free and being able to afford the things you want are great, the real win is the sense of confidence and security you gain. Knowing that you're not just blowing through your cash but are using it in a way that benefits you, supports your values, and prepares you for the future can make all the difference in how you view and manage your money. So, as we wrap up this chapter, remember that managing your finances responsibly isn't just about numbers and budgets; it's about crafting a lifestyle that reflects who you are and what you stand for, all while ensuring you're set for whatever lies ahead.

Financial Savvy Quiz

To check your understanding of financial terms and concepts, take this quick quiz! Jot down your answers and find out how financially literate you are:

1. Do you know what the envelope system is and how it helps manage cash? Yes / No

2. Have you tried using digital budgeting apps like Mint or YNAB to track your expenses? Yes / No

3. Are you aware of how compound interest works and how it can grow your savings over time? Yes / No

4. Do you practice mindful spending by reflecting on your emotional triggers and aligning your purchases with your goals? Yes / No

5. Do you understand the basics of filing taxes and how it impacts your earnings from part-time jobs or side hustles? Yes / No

Count your 'Yes' answers:

- 4-5 means you're a financial whiz!

- 2-3 suggests you're well on your way but could use a bit more fine-tuning.

- 1 or below? Let's boost your financial knowledge to ensure you're ready for financial success!

As we turn the page from mastering the basics of money management to exploring the exciting world of earning, remember that each step you take builds upon the last. The skills and habits you've developed here set the stage for the next chapter, where you'll learn not just to manage money, but make it grow. Ready to dive into the dynamic ways of earning and maximizing your financial potential? Let's get to it!

CHAPTER 3

DIVING INTO THE WORLD OF EARNING

You know that thrill when you unlock a new level in your favorite game? Imagine that, but with earning your own money. Yep, we're diving into the wild and sometimes wacky world of first jobs. It's like stepping into a whole new arena where the game rules are a bit different, and the rewards? Well, they're real money, not just digital coins or points. Whether you're saving for something big, or just want some extra cash to spend, landing your first job is a big deal. But before you can see that sweet paycheck, there's some groundwork to be laid. From crafting a killer resume to acing your job interviews, let's gear up and get you ready to score your first job like a pro.

3.1 First Job Fundamentals: What You Need to Know

Preparing for Job Applications

Alright, hero-in-training, your first quest is to create a resume. Think of your resume as your personal highlight reel. What have you done so far? Any school projects where you knocked it out of the park? Maybe you organized a charity event, or you're the captain of your soccer team? All of this goes in. Employers love seeing that you've taken the lead on projects or have committed to long-term activities, as it shows reliability and initiative—superhero qualities right there!

But here's the kicker—not all experiences need to be paid to be valuable. Volunteered at a local animal shelter? That counts. Helped out at your family business? Definitely counts. Each experience has given you a set of skills, whether it's communication, teamwork, problem-solving, or something else. Make sure to list these skills on your resume. Use bullet points to describe each role and responsibility, focusing on what you accomplished or learned in each position. This makes it easy for potential employers to see why you're the right fit for the job.

Interview Techniques

Moving on to the boss level: the job interview. Interviews can be nerve-wracking, but think of them as a friendly chat where both you and the interviewer are trying to see if you'd make a good team. To prepare, do a bit of homework on the company. What do they do? What's their culture like? Showing that you know your stuff can really impress.

Now, imagine some questions they might ask. Common ones include "Tell us about yourself," "What are your strengths and weaknesses?" or "Why do you want to work here?" Have some answers ready, but keep them natural. No one expects you to be perfect; they just want to see that you're enthusiastic and willing to learn.

Here's a pro tip: practice your answers with a friend or in front of a mirror. It might feel a bit silly, but it helps you get comfortable with what you want to say. And remember, interviews are a two-way street. Prepare a couple of questions to ask them—maybe about what a typical day looks like in the role, or what they like best about working there. This shows you're serious about the job and already thinking ahead.

Understanding Job Contracts

Got the job? High five! But before you start celebrating, let's talk paperwork—specifically, your job contract. This document is important because it outlines everything from your job duties to your salary, work hours, and other critical details like sick leave and vacation time. It's like the rulebook for your employment.

When you receive your contract, read it thoroughly. Yes, it might be as dry as your history textbook, but it's crucial to understand what you're agreeing to. Look out for things like the length of your probation period, conditions for termination, and any non-compete clauses that might restrict your work activities both during and after your employment. If something in the contract makes you go "huh?" don't hesitate to ask for clarification. It's better to ask questions now than face surprises later.

Workplace Rights and Responsibilities

Stepping into the workplace also means knowing your rights and responsibilities. You have the right to a safe and respectful working environment, free from harassment or discrimination. You're also entitled to be paid at least the minimum wage, so check what that is in your area. On your end, you're expected to perform your job duties to the best of your abilities and follow company policies and procedures. Think of it as being part of a team—everyone's got their part to play, and knowing the rules helps everyone succeed.

Navigating your first job can seem as tricky as trying to defeat a final boss in a game, but with the right prep, you'll not only survive but thrive. So, suit up with these tips, and get ready to earn not just money, but valuable experience that'll level you up for the future. Let's make that first job a grand slam!

3.2 Entrepreneurial Spirit: Starting Your Own Business as a Teen

So, you're eyeing the entrepreneurial lane, thinking you might just have the chops to start your own gig while juggling school work? That's the spirit! Starting a business as a teen isn't just about making some extra cash; it's about creating your own path and learning the ropes of real-world business early on. But what kind of business can you start with a shoestring budget and a full school schedule? Let's run through some cool ideas.

First, there's the classic tutoring service. If you ace your math tests or are a wizard with science experiments, why not leverage those skills? Tutoring younger students or peers can be a rewarding and profitable venture—and you're basically getting paid to reinforce what you know, which could even bump your own grades up. Next up, crafting. Yes, turning your hobby into cash. Whether it's jewelry, custom T-shirts, or even digital art, if you create it, chances are someone wants to buy it. Set up at local fairs or sell online. Then there's the ever-reliable car wash service. It's simple, requires minimal setup, and let's be honest, it's kind of fun. Plus, it's a great way to soak up some sun and stay active.

Got a few ideas buzzing? Great! Now, let's talk about laying the groundwork. Every solid business starts with a solid plan. Scribble down what you want to do, how you plan to do it, and what you expect to make. This doesn't have to be a Wall Street level business plan—just enough to guide you and keep you focused. Budgeting comes next. Figure out what you need to spend money on—supplies, advertising, maybe a website—and how much you can afford to spend. Remember, the goal is to make more money than you spend, so keep it lean.

Marketing your new business is crucial. You're not just selling a product or a service; you're selling yourself and your brand. Use social media to your advantage. It's free, it's effective, and let's face it, you're probably on it a lot anyway. Create engaging posts that showcase your products or services. Share behind-the-scenes glimpses of your creative process or fun facts about what you do. It's all about connecting with your audience and building relationships.

Now, the legal stuff—it's not the most thrilling part, but it's essential. Depending on where you live, there might be regulations to follow or permits to get, especially if you're handling food or running a business that requires you to be on public property. A quick chat with a local business counselor or a bit of online research can help you navigate this maze. Make sure you're clear on what's needed so your business is legit from the start.

Balancing school and business is like trying to finish homework while your favorite show is on. It takes discipline and a bit of clever time management. Set a schedule that allows you to focus on both without burning out. Maybe dedicate weekends or specific hours after school to your business. And don't forget to communicate with your family; they can be your biggest supporters, helping you balance your time or even stepping in when things get hectic.

Lastly, let's talk failure—a scary word, right? But here's the thing: many successful entrepreneurs faced setbacks before they hit it big. Failure is not the opposite of success; it's a part of the success story. It teaches resilience, sparks creativity, and builds character. Don't shy away from challenges. Embrace them. Learn from what went wrong and use that knowledge to come back stronger. Remember, every entrepreneur starts somewhere, and every empire starts with a single step—or misstep.

So, whether you're tutoring, crafting, or scrubbing cars, your teen business adventure is a fantastic way to learn, earn, and grow. Who knows? This small business could be the start of something big, paving the way to a future where you call the shots. Ready to get started? Let's do this!

3.3 Side Hustles for Teens: Making Money Online and Offline

So, you're interested in making some extra dough but maybe not ready to dive into a full-time job or start a mega business? That's where side hustles come into play. They're like the snack before dinner—satisfying, flexible, and can definitely keep you going! Whether you're tech-savvy and prefer the digital realm or more about that face-to-face interaction, there's a multitude of ways to pad your wallet. Let's explore some cool online and offline options that can get you started on your side hustle journey.

Exploring Online Opportunities

First off, the internet is like a treasure chest when it comes to earning opportunities. For starters, if you've got a knack for writing, graphic design, or even video editing, freelancing could be your golden ticket. Platforms like Upwork or Fiverr provide a space to showcase your skills and connect with clients from all over the globe. Imagine designing a logo for a startup on the other side of the world or writing articles for a travel blogger—all from the comfort of your room!

Then there's the realm of surveys and market research. Companies are always looking to get feedback on their products and are willing to pay for your thoughts. Sites like Survey Junkie or Swagbucks offer you a way to voice your opinions while earning some cash or gift cards. Sure, you're not going to buy a yacht with what you make here, but it's a simple way to earn while binge-watching your favorite series.

Content creation is another exciting avenue. Platforms like YouTube, Tik-Tok, or Instagram are not just for scrolling; they're potential money-makers. If you love sharing stories, teaching something, or just making people laugh, monetizing your content through ads or sponsorships could turn your hobby into a paying gig. Plus, it's a fantastic way to express yourself and connect with like-minded folks.

Offline Side Hustles

Prefer the tangible world? There's plenty of money to be made offline too. Classic side hustles like babysitting or pet sitting never go out of style. Start by offering your services to neighbors or family friends. Be reliable, do a great job, and word of mouth will take care of the rest. Flyers and local social media groups can also help expand your client base.

Or how about getting your hands dirty with some lawn mowing? It's a great workout and can be pretty lucrative, especially during the warmer months. Start with your own lawn to gain some experience, then reach out to neighbors or use local community boards to find clients. Offering to handle additional tasks like raking leaves or shoveling snow can turn this into a year-round gig.

Safety First

Whether online or offline, keeping safe is your number one priority. When interacting on digital platforms, safeguard your personal information. Use strong, unique passwords for every site, and think twice before sharing details like your home address or phone number. Be wary of scams—legitimate companies will never ask for payment from you to get a job or prize.

When working with new clients offline, especially in jobs like babysitting or pet sitting, safety comes first. Always have an initial meeting in a public place and if possible, bring a parent or another adult with you when meeting clients for the first time. Also, let someone know where you are, who you're with, and how long you expect to be there.

Financial Management of Earnings

Now, managing the money you earn from your side hustles is crucial. It's tempting to spend all that hard-earned cash, but wise management can help you save for bigger goals or cover unexpected expenses. Set up a system for tracking your income and expenses—it can be as simple as a spreadsheet or a dedicated app. This not only helps you stay organized but also gives you insights into how much you're really making after costs like travel or materials.

Consider setting aside a portion of every payment into a savings account. It's a good habit that builds your savings over time, plus it provides a financial cushion for slower months. Remember, regular small amounts add up to big savings eventually. This disciplined approach to money management can set you up for financial success well beyond your teenage years.

By exploring these varied side hustles and approaching them with safety and financial wisdom, you're not just earning some extra cash—you're also building valuable skills and habits that will benefit you throughout life.

Whether online or offline, there's a world of opportunities waiting for you to seize. So why not start today? Grab that opportunity, hustle smart, and watch as your efforts turn into tangible rewards.

3.4 Turning Passions into Profit: Monetizing Your Hobbies

Imagine transforming what you love doing in your downtime into a cool stream of income. Yes, that hobby that has you glued to your camera, gaming console, or notebook could actually be your ticket to earning some sweet cash. It's about tapping into that thing you're already passionate about and flipping it into a profitable venture. Let's get into how you can identify which of your hobbies could potentially rake in some money, how to gauge the market for it, find the right platforms to sell, and effectively promote it.

First things, first—identifying monetizable hobbies. The trick here is to look at your hobbies through a lens of profitability. For instance, if you're always snapping photos on your phone and have a good eye for lighting and composition, photography could be your goldmine. Or maybe you're a whiz at video games; streaming could be your thing. Love writing stories or poems? Consider freelance writing or publishing your work online. The key is to assess what you're good at and what you enjoy, then brainstorm how these can be turned into services or products. Think broadly; it's not just about selling physical goods. Offering a service or digital products can often have lower overheads and be just as profitable.

Now onto the nudge and nitty-gritty of market research. Before you dive in, you need to understand the demand for your hobby-turned-product or service. Start by checking out what's already out there. Who are your potential competitors? What are they offering, and at what price? Platforms like Instagram and Etsy can give you a feel for the market. Notice which related products or services get a lot of engagement or admiration. This can help you spot trends and figure out pricing strategies. Tools like Google Trends can also show you the search volume for keywords related to your hobby, indicating interest levels and seasonal spikes.

Choosing the right platforms is crucial in turning your hobby into a business. For physical products like handmade crafts or art prints, Etsy is a popular choice because it's tailored for independent creators and has a built-in audience that appreciates unique, handmade items. If you're into vintage finds or custom gadgets, eBay might be your arena, as it reaches a massive global market. For services like graphic design or writing, platforms like Fiverr can connect you with clients looking for freelance talent. If streaming is your game, Twitch or YouTube can be your stage, where engaging content could attract subscribers and advertisers.

Promoting your hobby effectively is the final piece of the puzzle. Utilizing social media is non-negotiable in today's digital age. It's not only free but also a powerful tool to reach a vast audience. Create engaging content that showcases your products or services. Use behind-the-scenes photos or videos, customer testimonials, and before-and-after shots to tell a story that resonates with your target audience. Don't shy away from using paid ads on these platforms once you've established what works—they can be a cost-effective way to reach potential customers. Additionally, learning the basics of SEO can help people discover your offerings through search engines, increasing your online visibility without breaking the bank.

By carefully assessing your hobbies for profitability, conducting thorough market research, choosing the right platforms, and effectively promoting your offerings, you can turn your passion into a paycheck. It's about leveraging what you already love to create a source of income that doesn't just feel like work. So, why not turn that hobby into a hustle? Your passion could very well be your next payday.

3.5 Understanding Taxes: What Happens to Your Earnings

Okay, so you've started making some money, and that's awesome. But here comes the part that might make you groan a bit—taxes. Yep, those inevitable deductions from your earnings that can seem like a total buzzkill. But hang on, they're not just some random chunk of your hard-earned cash getting swiped away. Taxes play a crucial role in, well, pretty much everything around us—from the roads you skate on to the schools you attend. So, let's break  down the basics of taxes, why they're important, and how you can handle them like a pro, even if it's your first time dealing with them.

First up, why do we even pay taxes? Imagine your community as a massive multiplayer online game. For the game to run smoothly, you need servers, maintenance folks, and regular updates, right? Taxes are like the subscription fee we all pay to keep our community—our real-life server—running smoothly. They help fund public services like emergency healthcare, education, public safety, and yes, even the roads and parks where you hang out. So, while it might sting to see a slice of your paycheck go towards taxes, remember, it's helping keep a lot of essential services up and running.

Now, let's talk about how you actually handle these taxes. When you start a job, you'll typically fill out a form called a W-4. This form tells your employer how much tax to withhold from your paycheck based on your financial situation. It's kind of like setting up the settings in a game—you're telling the system how to work best for you. Then, at the end of the year, you'll receive a W-2 form from your employer. This form summarizes how much you've earned and how much tax you've already paid. If you're freelancing or running your own gig, you might deal with a form called a 1099, which also details your earnings but doesn't include tax deductions, meaning you'll have to handle those yourself.

Filing a tax return is your next step. It might sound daunting, but it's basically just settling up with the government. It's how you tell them, "Here's what I made, here's what I owe in taxes, and here's what I've already paid." Sometimes, you might find out you've paid too much, and guess what? Hello, tax refund! That's money coming back to your pocket. Or, if you haven't paid enough, you'll need to cover the difference. There are plenty of free resources and software that can guide you through the process, making it less of a headache and more of a step-by-step walkthrough.

For you, as a teen, there are some specific tax deductions and credits that might be relevant. For instance, if you're working while attending school, you might qualify for education-related deductions. These can help lower the amount of taxable income you report, which can reduce your overall tax bill. There's also the possibility of deductions for self-employed expenses if you're hustling on the side, like costs for materials or even home office expenses. Keeping track of these expenses and knowing what deductions you're eligible for can make a significant difference in how much tax you end up paying.

Sometimes, especially if you're juggling a side business and your taxes start looking more complex, it might be wise to chat with a tax professional. They can offer guidance tailored to your specific situation, helping you navigate through the maze of tax laws and ensuring you get all the benefits you're entitled to. Think of them as a guide in a particularly tricky level of a game, where having some expert advice can help you come out on top.

Handling taxes responsibly sets you up not just for financial compliance, but also for financial success. By understanding how taxes work, making sure you're paying the right amount, and taking advantage of any deductions or credits, you're taking full control of your financial health. And while taxes might never be the most thrilling part of making money, understanding them can certainly make your financial journey a lot smoother. So, gear up with this knowledge, and tackle your taxes with confidence. After all, they're just another part of the game, and now you know how to play this level like a pro.

3.6 Paychecks and Allowances: Managing Your Income Wisely

So, you've landed your first job or you're pulling in a regular allowance from the ol' parents—congrats! You're on your way to financial independence. But before you start planning your spending spree, let's decode that paycheck you're so excited to cash. Understanding your paycheck is like knowing the rules of a new game. Your paycheck usually shows your gross income, which is your total earnings before any deductions. Think of it as your total score before any points are subtracted. Then, there are deductions—these can include taxes, Social Security, and maybe health insurance premiums if you've opted in. What you're left with after these deductions is your net income, or take-home pay. This is your spendable score, what you really have to play with.

Managing this money wisely is crucial, and it starts with smart allocation of your funds. If you're still getting allowances, this is a great practice field for budgeting. Think of your allowance as a mini-paycheck. How you use it can teach you a lot about managing bigger sums down the line. A good strategy is to divide your money into three parts: savings, spending, and sharing. It's up to you how you split it, but a balanced approach might look like putting 50% into savings, 40% into spending, and 10% into sharing or charitable acts. This method not only promotes healthy financial habits but also prepares you for handling larger finances in the future.

Prioritizing your financial goals is another key skill. Say you have several goals like saving for a new phone, buying a birthday gift for a friend, and contributing to a family outing. Not all goals are created equal, so you'll need to rank them based on importance and how soon you need the money. A priority list helps you focus on what's urgent and important, ensuring you meet your most critical goals first while setting aside funds for less immediate ones. This prioritization should reflect in your budgeting, influencing how you distribute your money across your various goals.

Parents can play a huge role in turning allowances into powerful learning tools. If you're a parent reading this, consider setting structured guidelines for how allowances should be spent and saved. Encourage your teens to budget their allowance by setting up jars or envelopes for different spending categories. This visual can help them see where their money is going and understand the consequences of their spending decisions. Regular discussions about money management can also help reinforce these lessons, turning everyday spending decisions into teachable moments.

Managing your money wisely isn't just about saving up for something big. It's about creating habits that will help you handle your finances effectively throughout your life. Whether it's understanding the breakdown of your paycheck, responsibly dividing your allowance, or setting and prioritizing financial goals, these skills lay the groundwork for financial savvy that extends far beyond your teenage years. And while money management might not be the most exhilarating of tasks, getting a handle on it early can lead to a future where your financial worries are minimized, and your opportunities are maximized. So, take these lessons to heart, start applying them to your daily financial decisions, and watch as your financial confidence grows.

Financial Savvy Quiz

To check your understanding of job fundamentals and preparation, take this quick quiz! Jot down your answers and find out how ready you are for your first job:

1. Do you know what types of unpaid experiences can be valuable to include on your resume? Yes / No

2. Have you practiced answering common interview questions like "Tell us about yourself" or "What are your strengths and weaknesses?" Yes / No

3. Do you understand what to look for and clarify in a job contract before signing it? Yes / No

4. Are you aware of your workplace rights, such as the right to a safe and respectful environment and being paid at least the minimum wage? Yes / No

5. Have you started thinking about questions to ask during a job interview to show your interest in the role and company? Yes / No

Count your 'Yes' answers:

- 4-5 means you're a job readiness whiz!

- 2-3 suggests you're well on your way but could use a bit more fine-tuning.

- 1 or below? Let's boost your job preparation knowledge to ensure you're ready for success!

As this chapter closes, I've equipped you with the tools to not only earn money but manage it with intelligence and foresight. You're now ready to step into the wider world of financial planning and investment—a world where you'll learn to make your money grow and work for you. Stay tuned, because next up, we're diving into the fundamentals of investing, where you'll start to turn your savings into significant capital that can fund your dreams. Let the adventure continue!

CHAPTER 4

CREDIT AND DEBT: NAVIGATING CHALLENGES

Picture this: You've just landed your dream gig at a trendy downtown café, and along with that first paycheck, you're feeling pretty flush. It's like you've hit the next level in a game where you've been grinding away for ages. Now, imagine you've got a shiny credit card or the option to take out a loan. Tempting, right? Suddenly, you can afford that killer guitar or the latest smartphone without waiting. But here's the catch—this isn't just free money. Welcome to the world of credit and debt, a place where you can either craft a catapult to launch you towards your financial goals or dig a pit that's tough to climb out of.

4.1 Credit Basics: What Is Credit and Why It Matters

Definition and Importance

So, what exactly is credit? Think of it as financial trust. It's the trust that financial institutions, like banks or credit unions, place on you to borrow their money and pay it back later. This trust is measured in several ways: consumer credit, revolving credit, and installment credit. Consumer credit is your general creditworthiness across the board—it's what you use for personal purchases. Revolving credit is like a pool of funds you can use, pay back, and use again—credit cards are a perfect example of this. Installment credit refers to loans with fixed payments and timelines, like your standard car loan or student loans.

Why does it matter? Credit is a cornerstone of modern economics. It allows you to spread the cost of big-ticket items over time, making it easier to afford things that might otherwise be out of reach. It's also crucial when you don't have the cash upfront for essential investments like furthering your education or buying a home. Managed wisely, credit can open doors to financial opportunities and stability.

Credit as a Financial Tool

When used smartly, credit isn't just about going on a shopping spree without immediate consequences. It's a strategic financial tool. For instance, say you're eyeing an advanced computer for your budding graphic design skills. Using a credit line responsibly to make this purchase can help you start earning money from freelance gigs long before you could save up enough to buy the computer outright. Similarly, student loans are often considered a worthwhile investment in your future earning potential. The key is to leverage these tools without overextending yourself—balance is everything.

Risks and Responsibilities

Now, for every superhero tool, there's a villain lurking around the corner. In the world of credit, that villain is debt—specifically, unmanageable debt. This happens when you borrow more than you can pay back, miss payments, or lose track of how much you owe. The consequences can include damaged credit scores, increased debt from interest and fees, and a whole lot of stress. Remember, with great borrowing power comes great responsibility. It's crucial to keep track of all your credit activities and make sure you're not signing up for more than what you can handle.

Building a Credit Philosophy

Here's where you get to put on your philosopher's hat. Developing a personal credit philosophy is about setting your own rules and boundaries when it comes to borrowing. Ask yourself: What do I believe is worth going into debt for? How much debt can I comfortably handle based on my current and expected future income? What are my financial goals, and how will credit help me achieve them? Your answers will guide your decisions and help you use credit as a powerful ally rather than a foe.

By understanding the basics of credit, recognizing it as a valuable financial tool, acknowledging the responsibilities that come with it, and developing a sound credit philosophy, you're laying down a solid foundation for financial savvy. Credit isn't just a way to get what you want now—it's a strategic resource that, when used wisely, can help pave the way to a financially sound future. So, think of it as a character in your personal finance saga—one that you need to understand and manage wisely as you write your own epic financial story.

4.2 The Truth About Credit Cards: Benefits and Traps for Teens

Let's talk plastic—no, not the kind you recycle, but credit cards, those little rectangles that can feel like a VIP pass to virtually anything. Before you swipe that card, though, it's crucial to understand exactly how they work. So buckle up, because you're about to get a crash course in Credit Cards 101. First off, every time you use a credit card, you're essentially borrowing money from the credit card company. You can spend up to a set limit (like a cap on how  much you can borrow at one time), and then you have the freedom to pay it back monthly. Sounds simple, right? But here's where it gets tricky: if you don't pay back the full amount by the due date, you'll be charged interest on whatever you still owe.

This brings us to the concept of a grace period, which is basically your new best friend. This is the time between the end of your billing cycle and the date your payment is due. If you pay your entire balance within this period, you won't be charged any interest. It's like the credit card company is saying, "Don't worry, take a minute to get your funds together." But if you miss that window, brace yourself for interest charges, which can accumulate faster than likes on a viral video.

Understanding interest rates is also key. These rates can vary wildly, and they determine how much extra you'll pay if you carry a balance. The higher the rate, the more money you'll shell out. Then there's the minimum payment—the lowest amount you can pay on your bill to avoid fees. It might be tempting to pay just this amount, but doing so means you'll rack up more interest on the remaining balance. Think of it like scooping water out of a boat with a leak; if you're not scooping fast enough, you're still going to sink eventually.

Now, despite these pitfalls, credit cards aren't all doom and gloom. When used wisely, they have some real perks. For starters, regularly using a credit card and paying it off in full can help you build a solid credit history, which is crucial for future financial moves like getting a loan or renting an apartment. Plus, many credit cards offer rewards programs—think cashback on purchases, points you can use for travel, or discounts at certain retailers. It's like getting a little bonus just for handling your money smartly.

But here's where many fall into a trap: overspending. Credit cards can make it feel like you've got more money than you actually do. It's easy to think, "I'll deal with it later," but this mindset can lead to debt that grows and becomes unmanageable. High interest rates and late fees can turn what was once a manageable amount into a financial nightmare faster than you might think.

To steer clear of these traps, adopt some smart credit card practices. First, always aim to pay your balance in full each month to avoid interest. Treat your credit card like a debit card; if you don't have the cash in your bank account, think twice before charging something. Next, keep a close eye on your statements. Regular reviews can help you spot any errors or fraudulent charges, plus it keeps you aware of your spending patterns. Set up alerts or check your account online to stay on top of your finances without waiting for your monthly statement.

Remember, a credit card is a tool, not a magic wand. Used responsibly, it can help you build your credit score and reap nice rewards. But mismanaged, it can become a financial burden. So, wield it wisely, enjoy the benefits, and stay in control of your spending. After all, your financial health is in your hands—and yes, sometimes in your wallet, too.

4.3 Good Debt vs. Bad Debt: Making Informed Choices

Ever felt that all debt is the same old monster under your financial bed, waiting to grab your wallet? Well, plot twist: not all debt is created equal. There's the good, the bad, and the ugly. Knowing how to tell them apart is like being able to spot the difference between a rip-off and a real deal.

Let's break down the difference between good debt and bad debt, because, believe it or not, some debts can actually work in your favor!

Defining Good and Bad Debt

First off, good debt is like a savvy investment in your future. It's the kind that helps you grow your net worth or generates income over time. Think of student loans—yes, the dreaded student loans. They might feel like a backpack full of bricks now, but they're often considered good debt because they're an investment in your education, boosting your earning power down the line. Then there's a mortgage. Buying a home can be a solid move since real estate generally appreciates over time, making it a classic case of good debt.

On the flip side, bad debt is the kind that doesn't increase your wealth or contribute to a significant life goal. It's like adding water to your gas tank; it just isn't going to help the engine run better! High-interest credit card debt is the poster child for bad debt. It's easy to rack up, the interest rates can be sky-high, and it usually funds the 'wants' not the 'needs'—like that latest smartphone or designer jeans that turn old in a season. This kind of debt can drag you down faster than sandbags on a hot air balloon.

Assessing the Value of Debt

So, how do you figure out if taking on a certain debt is a wise move? It's all about weighing the potential Return on Investment (ROI) and the interest rates. Say you're eyeing a loan for a top-notch coding bootcamp. It might set you back a few grand now, but if it significantly bumps up your job prospects and salary expectations, the ROI could be worth it. On the other hand, if you're borrowing money to splurge on a luxury vacation, the only return you're getting is a suntan and some Instagram likes, which, spoiler alert, won't pay off the debt.

Here's where things get real: always check the interest rates. They can either be your best buddy or that friend who always bails last minute. Low-interest rates can make a loan manageable and worth considering if the debt is for something that adds value to your life in the long run. But if the rates are high, you need to think twice, because the cost of borrowing might not justify the expense in the end.

Examples and Case Studies

Let's say Emma, a high school grad, takes out a student loan at a reasonable interest rate to pursue a degree in engineering—a field known for its solid salary packages. Fast forward a few years, and her degree helps her land a job that not only covers her living expenses but also allows her to pay back her loan comfortably. That's good debt at work.

Now, consider Jake. He whips out his credit card to buy the latest gaming console. It's fun, sure, but it doesn't exactly contribute to his financial growth. If Jake can't pay off that balance quickly, the interest starts building up, turning his cool new gadget into a financial burden. That's bad debt creeping in.

Strategic Borrowing

Strategic borrowing is about knowing when to take on debt and why. It's like choosing the right tool for the job. If debt can boost your future income or contribute significantly to your life goals (like education or a home), it's worth considering. But always align your borrowing with your financial capacity. Look at your current income, your job stability, and your future income potential. If a debt is manageable within those parameters and brings substantial value, it might just be a smart move.

Remember, every debt you take on is a slice of your future income that you're committing today. Make sure it's worth the trade-off. By understanding the differences between good and bad debt, assessing their value, learning from real-life examples, and thinking strategically about when and why to borrow, you're equipping yourself with the knowledge to make informed and beneficial financial decisions. So next time you face a borrowing decision, you'll be ready to distinguish whether it's a step towards building your wealth or just a pitfall in disguise.

4.4 Strategies to Avoid Debt: Practical Tips for Teens

Budgeting to Prevent Debt

Think of budgeting like planning your strategy in a multiplayer game—you need to know your resources, understand the terrain (your expenses!), and plan your moves (spending) so you don't end up wiped out (broke!). Setting up a budget isn't about restricting your fun; it's more about managing your funds smartly so you can have fun without the stress of debt hanging over your head. Here's the scoop on making budgeting your secret weapon against debt.

Start by tracking where your money is going each month. Yes, every single dollar! This might sound tedious, but it's like doing recon in a strategy game. You need to know where you stand before you can make a winning move. Once you've got a clear picture, categorize your spending. Essentials like food and transport? Non-negotiables. Weekly outings with friends? Important, but flexible. This clarity allows you to see potential areas to save in without feeling like you're cutting down on the fun.

Adjusting your budget to accommodate debt repayment is crucial if you're already dealing with some debts, like a credit card balance. Allocate a portion of your income to paying off your debts before you plan your spending on other things. It's tempting to think 'out of sight, out of mind', but the sooner you deal with debt, the less interest you'll pay in the long run, and the quicker you'll be free of it. If it helps, visualize your debt shrinking each month—it's a great motivator!

Emergency Funds

Now onto something super important that often gets overlooked: the emergency fund. This isn't just for adults with a thousand responsibilities; it's for anyone who spends money, including you. Why? Because life loves throwing surprises at us—like that sudden invite to a concert you can't miss, or more seriously, a cracked phone screen when you can't afford to be phone-less.

An emergency fund acts like your financial safety net, catching you when unexpected expenses try to throw you off your game. Start small if you have to—maybe set aside a bit of your allowance or part-time job income. Even a little stash can grow into a fund that saves you from reaching for a credit card and spiraling into high-interest debt when surprises pop up.

Informed Financial Decisions

Ever seen those ads promising amazing products with payments that are basically pocket change? Or what about those credit card offers that seem too good to be true? Here's where you need to put on your detective hat and do some digging. Always read the fine print—those tiny words at the bottom of the offer. They're tiny for a reason; they often contain important information about interest rates, fees, and other terms that can turn what looks like a great deal, into a terrible debt trap.

Becoming financially savvy means being a bit skeptical. Ask questions like: What's the interest rate after the introductory period? Are there any fees I should know about? What do online reviews say about this service or product? This might require some research, but it's better to spend a few minutes reading up than years regretting a bad financial decision.

Using Cash Instead of Credit

Here's a radical idea: what if you try using cash for most of your purchases, especially the discretionary ones? Using cash can feel like a throwback to a simpler time, but it's incredibly effective in controlling spending. When you physically hand over bills and see your wallet thinning, it hits differently than just swiping a card. It makes you more conscious of how much you're spending and on what.

This is where the envelope system comes into play (remember where you allocate cash for different spending categories?) and can be a game-changer. Once the 'fun money' envelope is empty, that's it—no more spending until you refill it. This method forces you to prioritize and think critically about each purchase. Plus, it's harder to get into debt when you're using real cash, as you can't spend what you don't have.

By embracing these strategies—smart budgeting, building an emergency fund, making informed financial decisions, and using cash—you can steer clear of debt or manage it more wisely. It's all about setting yourself up for financial success, keeping your spending in check, and ensuring you're prepared for whatever comes your way. So, take these tips, tweak them to fit your lifestyle, and start building a financial cushion that lets you enjoy life without the constant worry of debt.

4.5 Credit Scores Explained: Building a Good Credit History Early

Think of your credit score as the ultimate school report card that follows you far beyond graduation. Unlike the grades you get in school, which might land you in a good college or a cool internship, your credit score can affect how you buy a car, rent your dream apartment, or even the job you land in some cases. So, what is a credit score exactly? It's a number that tells lenders how trustworthy you are with money. The higher the score, the more financial cred  you've got. This little number is calculated based on a few key things: your payment history, how much credit you use compared to what you have (this is called credit utilization), and how long you've been using credit.

Let's start with payment history because it's the heavyweight champion in determining your score, making up about 35% of it. Every time you make a payment on time, it's like hitting a home run in the credit leagues. But every missed payment is like striking out. The key here is consistency; even one missed payment can cause your score to drop significantly. It's like in video games where maintaining a streak gets you bonus points, but you lose them all if you mess up once.

Next up is credit utilization, which is basically how much of your available credit you're using. Imagine you have a credit limit of $1,000; experts say you shouldn't use more than 30% of it, which in this case, is $300. Stay under this limit, and you're showing you can handle credit without maxing out, which lenders love to see. This part of the puzzle can be tricky when you're just starting because you might not get a very high limit. But here's a hack: you can ask for a higher limit as you show your reliability by making payments on time, or you can spread out your purchases across different cards to keep your utilization low.

Now, let's talk about the length of your credit history. Basically, the longer you've been using credit responsibly, the better. It shows lenders you have a track record of being reliable. It's like when you play a game—the more you play, the better you get, and the more the game rewards you. Starting to build credit early can give you a leg up, so consider becoming an authorized user on a parent's credit card. This lets you benefit from their credit history without the responsibility of making payments directly. But remember, you want to make sure they have good credit habits; otherwise, it could backfire.

Keeping an eye on your credit score is crucial, not just for keeping track of your financial health, but also to protect against identity theft and fraud. You'd be surprised how common it is for someone's personal info to be used to open fraudulent accounts. Regularly checking your credit report, which you can do for free annually at sites like AnnualCreditReport.com, can help you catch mistakes or suspicious activities early on. Think of it as doing a regular security check on your financial identity to ensure everything is as it should be.

Building and maintaining a good credit score isn't just about unlocking the ability to borrow more money. It's about creating opportunities for yourself that extend well beyond your teen years into your adult life. By managing your credit wisely from the start, you set yourself up for financial freedom and success that can make all the difference in achieving your dreams. So, treat your credit like a VIP—keep it secure, use it wisely, and watch as it opens doors to a brighter financial future.

4.6 Dealing with Debt: Steps to Take if You Owe Money

Let's face it, realizing you're in debt can feel like waking up to find your phone's been blowing up with missed messages—except these messages are bills, and they're all screaming for attention. The first step in tackling this mess? Embrace your inner adult and acknowledge the debt. Yep, it's time to pull those bills out from under your bed or wherever you've been stashing them. Lay everything out on the table and get a clear picture of what you owe, to whom, and by when. It might sting a bit to see the total, but just like ripping off a Band-Aid, it's the first step to healing your finances.

Now, let's talk strategy—how are you going to pay this off? There are a couple of popular methods: the debt snowball and the debt avalanche. Think of the debt snowball as the feel-good strategy. You start small, paying off your smallest debt first while making minimum payments on the others. Each debt you pay off gives you more money (and motivation) to tackle the next one, snowballing your way out of debt. It's like leveling up in a game; each level you beat pumps you up to take on the next.

On the other hand, the debt avalanche is for the mathematically minded. This method focuses on paying off the debt with the highest interest rate first, while still making minimum payments on the others. It might not give you the quick wins of the snowball method, but it's efficient and saves you money on interest in the long run. It's like playing the long game in chess, making strategic moves that set you up for a better position several turns later.

Negotiating with creditors can also be a game-changer. If the idea of calling up your creditors gives you a mini heart attack, take a deep breath—you got this. Creditors often have options like payment plans or lower interest rates that they can offer to help you manage your payments better. When you call, be honest about what you can realistically afford to pay each month. It's like negotiating in a marketplace; if you don't ask, you won't get. Plus, showing that you're proactive can work in your favor, as creditors are more likely to help customers who are making an effort to pay their debts.

Sometimes, though, the debt might be too much to handle on your own, and that's okay. That's when bringing in a professional—like a financial advisor or a credit counseling service—can really help. These pros can offer you advice, help you set up a budget, and sometimes even negotiate with creditors on your behalf. Think of them as your financial guides, leading you through the tricky terrain of debt management. They can provide a roadmap out of debt, ensuring you don't take any wrong turns along the way.

Remember, getting into debt didn't happen overnight, and getting out of it won't either. But with acknowledgment, a solid repayment strategy, some savvy negotiating, and possibly some professional guidance, you can work your way towards a debt-free life. It's not just about clearing your debts; it's about setting yourself up for a financially healthy future where you can make choices based on what you want, not what you owe. So take that first step, choose your strategy, and start your journey back to financial freedom.

Financial Savvy Quiz

To check your understanding of financial terms and concepts, take this quick quiz! Choose the correct answer for each question:

1. **What is consumer credit?**

   - a) Credit used for business purchases

   - b) General creditworthiness used for personal purchases

   - c) Loans with fixed payments and timelines

2. **Which of the following is an example of revolving credit?**

   - a) Student loans

   - b) Car loans

   - c) Credit cards

3. **What is a grace period in terms of credit cards?**

   - a) The time you have to repay your balance before interest is charged

   - b) The minimum payment due each month

   - c) The maximum credit limit allowed

4. **What is considered 'bad debt'?**

   - a) Mortgage loans

   - b) High-interest credit card debt

   - c) Student loans

5. **What makes up the largest portion of your credit score?**

   - a) Payment history

   - b) Credit utilization

   - c) Length of credit history

Count your correct answers:

- 5 means you're a credit whiz!

- 4-3 suggests you're well on your way but could use a bit more fine-tuning.

- 2 or below? Let's boost your credit knowledge to ensure you're ready for financial success!

Answers:

1. b) General creditworthiness used for personal purchases

2. c) Credit cards

3. a) The time you have to repay your balance before interest is charged

4. b) High-interest credit card debt

5. a) Payment history

As we wrap up this chapter on navigating the challenges of credit and debt, remember that understanding and managing your financial obligations is crucial to maintaining and enhancing your financial health. Whether it's using credit wisely, strategizing debt repayment, or seeking professional advice, the choices you make today will shape your financial landscape tomorrow. Next up, we'll explore the exciting world of investing, where you'll learn how to grow your savings and potentially increase your wealth. Ready to take your financial knowledge to the next level? Let's dive in!

"Money can't buy happiness, but giving it away can." - Freddie Mercury

Hey there, future financial wizard! Did you know that people who give without expecting anything in return often lead happier, more successful lives? Pretty cool, right? And today, I want to share that awesomeness with you.

So, here's something to think about...

Would you be willing to help someone you've never met, even if you never got credit for it?

Who is this person you ask? They are like you. Or, at least, like you used to be. Less experienced, wanting to make a difference, and needing help, but not sure where to look.

Our mission is to make personal finance accessible to everyone. Everything I do stems from that mission. And, the only way for me to accomplish that mission is by reaching...well...everyone.

This is where you come in. Most people do, in fact, judge a book by its cover (and its reviews). So here's my ask on behalf of a struggling teen you've never met:

Please help that teen by leaving this book a review.

Your gift costs no money and less than 60 seconds to make real, but can change a fellow teen's life forever. Your review could help...

...one more student understand how to save money.
...one more young person learn to budget like a pro.
...one more teenager start investing early.
...one more dream of financial independence come true.

To get that 'feel good' feeling and help this person for real, all you have to do is...and it takes less than 60 seconds...
leave a review.

Simply scan the QR code below (or click the link for ebook) to leave your review:

[https://www.amazon.com/review/review-your-purchases/?asin=B0D9MX7BZN]

If you feel good about helping a faceless teen, you are my kind of person. Welcome to the club. You're one of us.

I'm that much more excited to help you master your finances faster and easier than you can possibly imagine. You'll love the tips and strategies I'm about to share in the coming chapters.

Thank you from the bottom of my heart.

- Your biggest fan, E.J. Goldwyn

CHAPTER 5

INVESTING FOR BEGINNERS

E ver felt like your piggy bank just isn't cutting it anymore? Like, sure, it's cute and all, but it's not exactly the powerhouse of wealth accumulation you need for those big dreams, right? Welcome to Investing 101, where your money doesn't just sit around eating chips; it actually gets a job and makes you more money. It's like turning your cash into a team of hardworking minions, all geared up to multiply and conquer the financial world for you. Let's dive into the magic of compound interest, the hero of our story, and see how it can transform small, regular investments into a hefty treasure chest over time.

5.1 Why Invest? Understanding the Power of Compound Interest

Explaining Compound Interest

So, compound interest—sounds complicated, but it's actually your best pal in the world of investing. Here's the scoop: compound interest is what happens when your investments earn money... and then that money earns more money. It's like a snowball rolling down a snowy hill, picking up more snow and getting bigger as it rolls along. You start with a small amount, and as it rolls through the years, it grows exponentially because you're earning returns  not just on your initial investment, but also on the returns that investment has already generated.

Imagine you invest $100, and it earns 10% interest annually. After the first year, you don't just have your original $100; now you've got $110. That extra $10 then starts earning interest too. So, the next year, you're not earning interest on just that $100—you're earning it on $110, which means you end up with $121. And it just keeps growing from there. The longer you leave it, the bigger it grows, and the faster it grows too!

Illustrative Examples

Let's break this down with some real-life scenarios to see just how powerful compound interest can be. Say, two teens decide to invest. Teen A starts at age 15, putting away $100 a month at an interest rate of 5% annually until age 65. Teen B waits until they're 35 to start saving the same amount, $100 a month, at the same interest rate until age 65.

Here's the kicker: Teen A, who started earlier, ends up with approximately $266,865 by age 65, compared to Teen B who only has about $83,225. That's the power of compound interest—starting early can result in a much bigger payoff because the interest has more time to do its magic.

Comparative Analysis

Now, imagine if Teen A didn't invest and just stuffed their money under a mattress. Sure, they'd still have the initial amount they saved, but by not investing, they'd miss out on all that potential growth from compound interest. It's like choosing to walk instead of taking a super-fast bike that's available to you. Why would you, right?

Long-Term Perspective

This brings us to the golden rule of investing: the long-term perspective. Investing isn't about making a quick buck; it's about setting up your future self for success. The earlier you start, the better off you'll be, thanks to compound interest. It's about playing the long game, watching your money grow, and planning for big future goals, whether that's college, a dream car, or even early retirement.

Investing might seem daunting at first, like stepping into a vast, mysterious forest where the paths aren't clearly marked. But once you understand the basics, especially the magic of compound interest, you start to see that each step you take, no matter how small, leads you towards a more secure and prosperous future. So, why not start now? Your future millionaire self will thank you.

5.2 Stocks and Bonds: Investment Basics for Teens

Okay, let's chat about stocks and bonds—your potential golden tickets to making your money work for you while you chill with friends or binge-watch your favorite series. Think of stocks and bonds as the bread and butter of the investing world. When you own a stock, you own a little piece of a company, like a slice of a giant corporate pizza. If the company does well, your slice could become more valuable, and you might get a share of the profits through dividends. Bonds, on the other hand, are more like lending your money to a company or government, and in return, they promise to pay you back with interest over a set period. It's like giving a loan to your friend who needs to buy a bike and agreeing they'll pay you back with a little extra for your trouble.

Now, how on earth do you start investing in these? Well, if you're under 18, you'll likely need to set up what's called a custodial account. This is an account your parents or another guardian can help you open. They'll manage it, but the money and investments are all yours. It's a way to dip your toes into the investing pool under the watchful eyes of someone with a bit more financial experience. You can buy stocks in companies you believe in or bonds that seem reliable, all through this account. It's a fantastic way to learn the ropes of investing with a safety net in place.

Let's talk about risks and rewards because, like all good things, investing comes with its fair share of ups and downs. Stocks can be a bit of a rollercoaster ride; they can increase in value quickly, but they can also drop just as fast. That's the thrill and the risk of the stock market. Bonds are generally more like a gentle carousel—less dramatic ups and downs but typically offering more stable and predictable returns. Both are valuable, but how you mix them can depend a lot on what kind of financial ride you're comfortable with.

Here are some practical tips to keep in your back pocket: First, do your homework. Look into companies or governments you're thinking of investing in. Are they stable? Do they have a good track record? It's a bit like checking the reviews before you buy a game or a gadget. You want to know what you're getting into. Also, diversification is your best friend in investing. Don't put all your eggs in one basket. Spread your investments across different types of assets—stocks, bonds, maybe even some real estate or mutual funds. This way, if one investment dips, you've got others to balance it out.

Remember, investing isn't just about making money quickly. It's about setting the stage for your financial future. By starting young, you're giving yourself a huge advantage. You have time to learn from mistakes, recover from dips, and watch your investments grow. So, why not start exploring the possibilities? With a bit of guidance, some smart choices, and a willingness to learn, you can begin to navigate the investing world with confidence.

5.3 Mutual Funds and ETFs: Diversifying Your Investments

Okay, so imagine you're at the coolest buffet ever. Instead of choosing just one dish, you get to load your plate with a bit of everything. That's kind of how mutual funds and ETFs (Exchange-Traded Funds) work. They bundle up a bunch of different investments—like stocks, bonds, and other goodies—into one package. This mix helps you spread out your risk and potentially increase your returns without putting all your eggs in one basket. Let's unwrap these two popular investment types and see how they can spice up your investment portfolio.

Definition and Differences

First off, mutual funds are like a big investment potluck. When you buy shares in a mutual fund, you're pooling your money with lots of other investors. This collective cash is managed by a pro who decides what to buy or sell based on the fund's goals. Think of it as having a chef who makes sure everyone at the party gets a well-balanced plate, without anyone needing to cook.

ETFs, on the other hand, are a bit different. They're also pooled investments, but they trade on stock exchanges just like individual stocks. This means you can buy and sell shares of ETFs throughout the trading day at changing prices, just like you would with stocks. Imagine a buffet where you can see the price of each dish changing based on how popular it is; that's kind of like trading ETFs.

Both mutual funds and ETFs offer a diverse mix, but the key difference lies in how they're managed and traded. Mutual funds are typically actively managed by financial experts who try to outperform the market, which might mean higher fees due to all that expert tinkering. ETFs, however, are usually passively managed and simply aim to mirror the performance of a specific index, like the S&P 500, which often leads to lower fees.

Benefits of Diversification

Now, why should you even consider diversifying your investments? Well, think about it this way: if you only invest in one company or one type of asset, it's like betting all your money on one horse in a race. If that horse doesn't perform well, you're in for a disappointment. But if you spread your bets across multiple horses, your risk of losing it all on one bad bet goes down.

That's exactly what mutual funds and ETFs do. They make it easy to own a small piece of many investments. If one stock or bond in the fund tanks, you're better protected because the other investments in the fund can help balance things out. This not only minimizes your risk but also stabilizes your returns over the long haul. It's like having a safety net while you're learning the ropes of the investing circus.

How to Invest in Mutual Funds and ETFs

Getting started with mutual funds and ETFs isn't as daunting as it might seem. For mutual funds, you often invest directly with a mutual fund company, and there's usually a minimum investment amount, which can vary from a few hundred to a few thousand dollars. You'll want to read the fund's prospectus, which is a document that details everything about the fund, including its objectives, fees, and the types of assets it includes. Think of it as the recipe book that tells you exactly what's in the meal you're considering.

For ETFs, since they trade like stocks, you'll need a brokerage account. You can buy and sell ETF shares throughout the trading day at current market prices. This can be a great way to start investing with relatively small amounts of money, especially if you opt for a brokerage that offers fractional shares, where you can buy a portion of a single ETF share.

Case Studies

Consider this: Emily, a college student, decided to invest in a mutual fund focusing on tech companies. She liked the idea of having an expert manage her investment, especially since she was busy with classes. Over a few years, even with the tech market's ups and downs, her initial investment grew thanks to the fund's diversification across various tech firms.

Then there's Jay, who chose an ETF that tracked the S&P 500. He appreciated the lower fees and the flexibility to buy and sell shares anytime during market hours. Over time, Jay's investment mirrored the overall market's performance, which historically has trended upwards, helping him build a solid nest egg.

Both Emily and Jay benefited from diversification, but they chose different paths that suited their individual needs and lifestyles. Whether you lean towards the curated experience of mutual funds or the DIY nature of ETFs, these tools can offer a practical route to achieving your financial goals, making them essential contenders in your investment strategy playbook.

5.4 Retirement Accounts for Teens: Thinking Ahead

Let's talk about retirement accounts. Yeah, I know, retirement feels like a zillion years away—like, somewhere between the invention of flying cars and teleportation. But here's the scoop: starting to think about retirement now, even as a teen, is like planting a tiny seed that will grow into a gigantic, shade-giving, fruit-bearing tree by the time you're ready to chill out and enjoy it. Retirement accounts, such as Roth IRAs, are specially designed pots where this magic growth happens. They're not just for old folks; they're financial tools that anyone, including you, can use to build a cushy financial cushion for the future.

First up, let's break down what a Roth IRA is all about. It's a type of retirement account where you put in money that's already been taxed (like the cash from your part-time job), and then—this is the cool part—it grows tax-free. You can pull out your contributions anytime without penalties, and if you wait until retirement age (59½), you can withdraw the earnings (that's the growth part) tax-free too. It's like putting your money in a magic box: the more time it spends in there, the more it multiplies, and when you finally open it, there's a lot more than what you put in!

Advantages of Early Investing

Now, why start so early? Imagine two gamers: one starts leveling up at the beginning of summer, and the other waits until winter break. By the time winter rolls around, the first gamer has a major advantage, right? It's the same with investing. The earlier you start, the more time your money has to grow thanks to the magic of compound interest (yup, that old friend). Plus, starting young means you can invest smaller amounts and still end up with a hefty sum. It's all about giving your money the maximum amount of time to work its magic.

How to Open a Retirement Account

So, how do you get this magic money pot, aka a Roth IRA? If you're under 18, you'll need an adult to help set up what's called a custodial Roth IRA. It's pretty much like any other Roth IRA, but your parent or guardian holds the reins until you're of age. They can help you open an account at most banks or investment firms. You'll need some basic info like your Social Security number and some cash to start—many accounts have a minimum amount to open, but it's usually not too hefty.

Once it's set up, you can start funneling some of your earnings from that summer job or even birthday money into it. Just keep in mind there's a limit to how much you can contribute each year, so check the latest figures to stay in the know. And here's a pro tip: set up automatic transfers to your Roth IRA to keep your savings consistent and hassle-free. It's like setting a video game to update automatically—you just sit back and reap the benefits without having to remember to do it manually.

Saving Versus Investing for Retirement

Now, let's clear up a common mix-up: saving vs. investing for retirement. Stashing cash under your mattress or even in a regular savings account is saving. It's safe, but it doesn't grow much. Investing, on the other hand, is putting that money into things like stocks, bonds, or mutual funds through your retirement account. Yes, investing comes with risks, but it also comes with the potential for much greater growth, especially over many years.

Think of it this way: if saving is like keeping your gaming gear clean and protected, investing is like using that gear to compete in tournaments where you can win big. Sure, you might face some tough matches, but the potential rewards are much higher. With a Roth IRA, you're essentially entering the long-game tournament of your financial future, equipped with the best gear (your investments) to help you win big (a comfy retirement).

So, even though retirement seems like it's eons away, setting up and starting to contribute to a retirement account now can be one of the smartest moves you make. It's about playing the long game, where patience, consistency, and a bit of strategic thinking set you up for a winning future. And hey, who says you can't have fun while planning for the future? Watching your investments grow is pretty satisfying, kind of like leveling up in your favorite game, knowing that each step forward gets you closer to that epic win. So why not get started? Your future self will definitely thank you for getting a head start on this whole retirement thing.

5.5 Risk and Return: Finding Your Investment Comfort Zone

Alright, let's talk about risk and return, which, in the investing world, are pretty much like the dynamic duo of your favorite superhero team. Understanding this relationship is crucial because it helps you navigate the investment landscape more like a pro surfer riding the waves rather than a newbie wiping out. So, here's the scoop: generally, the higher the risk of losing your money in an investment, the higher the potential return. It's like when you're gaming; the harder the level, the bigger the payoff (or epic fail). Conversely, lower-risk investments usually offer smaller returns, kind of like sticking to the easy levels and collecting fewer points.

Imagine you're considering two different investment options. One is a government bond, which is pretty safe but offers lower returns. The other is a stock in a new tech startup; it could skyrocket and make you the next teen millionaire, or it could flop, leaving you with zip. Here, the bond is your low-risk, low-return option, and the stock is your high-risk, high-return gamble. Deciding between the two depends on how much risk you're comfortable taking, which leads us to your personal risk tolerance.

Assessing your risk tolerance is like figuring out what kind of roller coasters you're okay with. Are you a 'loop-the-loop' thrill-seeker or a 'merry-go-round' chill rider? This isn't just about gut feelings; it's about considering your financial goals, time horizon, and emotional comfort. Your financial goals are what you're saving up for, like a car or college. Your time horizon is how long you can keep your money invested before you need it. And your emotional comfort? Well, that's how much financial ups and downs you can handle without losing sleep. If watching the stock market's daily gyrations is going to stress you out, high-risk investments might not be your jam.

Balancing risk and return in your investment portfolio is like mixing the perfect track in music production. You've got to adjust the levels and effects to create a harmonious sound. In investing terms, this means adjusting how much money you put into high-risk versus low-risk investments. A well-balanced portfolio typically includes a mix of both, which helps you manage risk while still aiming for a decent return. Techniques for maintaining this balance include rebalancing your portfolio regularly to ensure it aligns with your risk tolerance and investment goals. As your life changes—say, you get closer to needing the money for college—you might shift more into lower-risk investments.

Now, for the tech-savvy teens, there are some pretty cool online tools and simulators that can help you visualize potential investment outcomes. These platforms let you create virtual portfolios and see how different investments might perform over time, based on historical data. It's like playing a strategy game where you can test out various tactics without any real-world risk. You get to see a range of outcomes based on different levels of risk and can tweak your investment mix to see how it affects potential returns. Using these tools can give you a clearer picture of how different investments work and help you make more informed decisions about where to put your money.

In the grand scheme of things, understanding and managing the risk-return relationship in your investments is key to building a portfolio that not only grows but also fits your personal financial style. Whether you're just starting out with a few dollars from birthday money or looking to grow a more significant sum, knowing how to balance risk and reward is essential. It's all about making smart choices that align with your goals, timeline, and comfort zone, setting you up for financial success now and in the future. So, why not dive into these concepts, explore some investment simulations, and start crafting a strategy that works for you? Your future self will surely thank you for getting a head start on mastering the art of investment.

5.6 Tech and Investing: Digital Platforms for Teen Investors

Hey, let's talk tech and investing, because let's face it, even your grandma is texting emojis and streaming shows nowadays, so why shouldn't your investments be just as plugged in? The world of investing has seriously leveled up with digital platforms that are not just super user-friendly but are also packed with all the tools a budding investor could dream of. We're talking about platforms that make jumping into the investing pool as easy as downloading an app on your phone.

First up, let's walk through some of the coolest features these platforms offer. Think automated investing where, after setting up your preferences and goals, the platform takes over the tedious task of managing your investments. It's like having a financial advisor who doesn't sleep or take breaks. Then there are the low fees. Traditional investment brokers might charge you an arm and a leg, but many digital platforms offer low or even no fees for basic services, which is perfect when you're just starting and every penny counts. Plus, they come loaded with educational resources. We're talking tutorials, articles, and even quizzes that turn you from a newbie into a savvy investor, all at your own pace.

The convenience of these platforms can't be overstressed. Imagine being able to check your investments, make trades, and see real-time data anytime, anywhere—right from your phone. This accessibility makes it super easy to stay engaged with your investments and make informed decisions quickly. Starting small is also a big plus. Many of these platforms allow you to start investing with just a few dollars. Think of it as the financial equivalent of starting a new game at an easy level—you can get going without much upfront, learning as you grow.

But with great power comes great responsibility, right? So let's chat about keeping your money safe while investing online. Cybersecurity is a big deal because, unfortunately, the internet is also a playground for hackers. Protecting your personal information starts with the basics like using strong, unique passwords for your investment accounts, not sharing sensitive info, and always logging out after you use an app or website. It's also smart to enable two-factor authentication whenever available, adding an extra layer of security.

Choosing a secure platform is just as crucial. Stick to well-known, reputable platforms that use strong encryption to protect your data. Do your homework by reading reviews and checking their security protocols. If something about a platform feels off, trust your gut and steer clear. Remember, investing online is like venturing into a vast digital city—it's exciting and full of opportunities, but you always want to keep your wits about you.

Lastly, while these platforms make investing straightforward, it's important not to get carried away by the ease of use. Responsible investing means doing your research and understanding what you're getting into. Don't let the thrill of the 'buy' button lead you to make impulsive decisions that could hurt your finances. Think of each investment like a level in a game where strategy, not just speed, is key to winning.

So, as you dive into the digital investing scene, remember to balance the excitement of new tech with the wisdom of old-school financial prudence. Use the tools at your disposal to learn, grow, and gradually build your investment portfolio. This approach not only ensures you make the most of what tech has to offer but also protects you and your hard-earned money as you navigate the ever-evolving world of investments. And who knows? With the right mix of tech-savviness and investment wisdom, you might just be the financial superhero of your own story.

Financial Savvy Quiz

To check your understanding of financial terms and concepts, take this quick quiz! Choose the correct answer for each question:

1. **How does compound interest impact investments?**

   - A) It decreases the value of investments over time.

   - B) It has no effect on investment growth.

   - C) It causes investments to grow exponentially over time.

   - D) It stabilizes investment returns.

2. **What is the primary difference between stocks and bonds?**

   - A) Stocks are backed by governments, while bonds are issued by corporations.

   - B) Stocks offer fixed interest payments, while bonds represent ownership in a company.

   - C) Stocks provide ownership in a company, while bonds are debt instruments.

   - D) Stocks have guaranteed returns, while bonds are subject to market fluctuations.

3. **Why is starting to invest early beneficial?**

   - A) It reduces taxes on investments.

   - B) It allows more time for compound interest to grow investments.

   - C) It guarantees higher returns on investments.

   - D) It minimizes the risk of investment losses.

4. **Which account type requires an adult to manage until the account holder reaches legal age?**

   - A) Custodial account

   - B) Roth IRA

- ○ C) Traditional IRA

- ○ D) 401(k)

5. How does diversification help manage investment risk?

- ○ A) By guaranteeing high returns in all market conditions.

- ○ B) By focusing investments on a single asset type.

- ○ C) By spreading investments across different types of assets.

- ○ D) By ensuring investments remain liquid at all times.

Score interpretation:

- **5** correct answers: You're a financial whiz!

- **4-3** correct answers: You're well on your way but could use a bit more fine-tuning.

- **2 or below**: Let's boost your financial knowledge to ensure you're ready for financial success!

Answers:

1. c) It causes investments to grow exponentially over time.

2. c) Stocks provide ownership in a company, while bonds are debt instruments.

3. b) It allows more time for compound interest to grow investments.

4. a) Custodial account

5. c) By spreading investments across different types of assets.

As this chapter wraps up, remember that the fusion of technology and investing offers a dynamic platform for you to engage with financial markets actively. These digital tools empower you with real-time data, diversified investment options, and the flexibility to start small and grow over time. Embrace this new age of investing, but always with a cautious and informed approach. As we pivot to the next chapter, keep in mind that your financial journey is about blending innovation with sound financial practices to achieve your long-term goals. Let's keep the momentum going and continue building a robust financial foundation for your future.

CHAPTER 6

MODERN MONEY: DIGITAL FINANCE AND TRENDS

Ever felt like you're living in a sci-fi movie when you use your phone to check your bank balance or zap some cash to a friend? Welcome to the era of digital banking, where traditional piggy banks are becoming as outdated as floppy disks. Today, we're not just going digital; we're living digital. But as you navigate this high-speed world of bytes and blockchain, it's crucial to know how to manage your digital dough effectively. So, let's decode digital banking, explore its perks, dive into choosing the right digital bank, and walk through setting up your first account. Buckle up, because managing money is about to get a whole lot cooler (and easier)!

6.1: The Rise of Digital Banking: What Teens Need to Know

Understanding Digital Banking

First off, what is digital banking? Think of it as traditional banking's tech-savier sibling. Instead of walking into a building with fancy columns and waiting in line to talk to a teller, digital banking lets you handle all your financial transactions online. This could be through a website or more likely, an app on your phone. You can check balances, transfer money, pay bills, and more—all while lounging in your PJs at home.

But there's more. Have you heard of digital-only banks? These are banks without any physical branches. Yep, they exist entirely online. Then there are app-based banking solutions—these are services that might not be full-on banks but offer banking services directly through their apps. They're like pop-up shops for your finances, providing super convenient access without the need for a traditional bank account.

Benefits of Digital Banking

Now, why should you even care about digital banking? For starters, it's all about accessibility. You can manage your money anytime, anywhere, right from your smartphone or computer. Midnight snack runs can totally include checking your savings goals if that's your thing. Also, digital banks often have lower fees than traditional banks because they don't have the same overhead costs (no fancy buildings or lots of staff to pay). This means you can save on those annoying account maintenance fees or transaction charges.

Plus, digital banks are usually ahead of the curve when it comes to cool, innovative features. Ever wished you could set up a savings goal for that new game or concert ticket and see your progress? Many digital banking apps offer features just like that, making saving feel more like a fun challenge rather than a chore.

Choosing a Digital Bank

Choosing the right digital bank is like picking the right character in a video game—each has its own strengths and special abilities. Here's what to look for: Security features are top of the list because you definitely don't want your money to be as accessible to hackers as it is to you. Look for banks that offer two-factor authentication, encryption, and other security measures. Customer service is also key. Even though everything's online, sometimes you just need to talk to a human. Make sure the bank has a solid reputation for customer support—check out reviews and see what other users are saying.

Also, consider the range of services offered. Some digital banks offer just the basics, while others might provide additional perks like budgeting tools or automatic savings options. Think about what's important to you in managing your money and choose accordingly.

Getting Started with Digital Banking

Ready to jump into the world of digital banking? Setting up an account is usually pretty straightforward. You'll need some basic info like your name, address, and Social Security number. Some banks might also require a photo ID, which you can usually snap and upload using your phone. Make sure to read through the terms and conditions—yes, it can be tempting to skip this part, but it's important to know what you're signing up for, especially when it comes to fees or how your personal information is used.

Once your account is set up, take some time to explore the app or website. Set up security features like a strong password and two-factor authentication right away. Then, dive into setting up your financial dashboard. Many apps allow you to customize your main screen so you can easily check your most important accounts or savings goals at a glance.

And just like that, you're ready to manage your money like a pro, digitally. With these tools at your fingertips, you're not just prepared for the future of banking; you're riding the wave right at the forefront. Welcome to modern money management, where your financial freedom is literally in your hands. Let's make the most of it!

6.2 Cryptocurrencies: An Introduction for Teens

So, you've probably heard of Bitcoin, right? Maybe seen some wild headlines about people making millions – or losing it – overnight? Welcome to the electrifying world of cryptocurrencies, where finance meets technology in a revolutionary way. But before you think about jumping into this digital gold rush, let's unpack what cryptocurrencies really are, how they work, and what you need to know to navigate this high-tech financial frontier.

Cryptocurrencies are basically digital money, but unlike the traditional bucks in your bank account, they operate independently of a central financial authority like a government or bank. The tech behind this independence is called blockchain. Imagine a blockchain as a digital ledger, sort of like a super-advanced spreadsheet, spread across countless computers all over the world. Every transaction made with a cryptocurrency is recorded on this ledger, verified by a network of computers (called nodes), and then added as a new "block" to the chain of previous transactions. It's ultra-secure because to mess with one block, you'd have to mess with all the blocks on the chain in multiple places at once, which is practically impossible.

Let's talk about some of the big names in crypto. Bitcoin, the OG of cryptocurrencies, is the first and most well-known. It was created by an unknown person (or group of people) using the pseudonym Satoshi Nakamoto back in 2009 as a way to make transactions without the need for a middleman. Then there's Ethereum, another heavy hitter, known for its ability to execute smart contracts – these are contracts that automatically enforce themselves when certain conditions are met, all without any human intervention. And there are thousands of others, from Ripple to Litecoin to Cardano, each with its own unique features and uses.

Now, using cryptocurrencies isn't just about investing or trading; it's also about spending. More and more businesses, from big names like Microsoft and Starbucks to local cafes and online stores, are starting to accept cryptocurrencies as payment. This means you could buy your next video game or coffee using Bitcoin. It's a cool way to use digital money in the real world, and it's growing more common by the day.

However, with great technology comes great responsibility, and there are some risks you should be aware of. Cryptocurrencies can be wildly volatile. Their value can skyrocket one day and plunge the next. This makes them a risky investment – think of them more like a rollercoaster ride at an amusement park, not a gentle merry-go-round. It's crucial to understand that investing in cryptocurrencies isn't a guaranteed way to make money and you should only invest what you can afford to lose.

Moreover, the world of cryptocurrencies is still relatively new and is not as regulated as traditional banking. This can be a double-edged sword. On one hand, it offers freedom from traditional financial systems; on the other, it can be a bit like the Wild West, with fewer safeguards in place. That's why doing your homework, understanding the risks, and proceeding with caution is key. Whether you're thinking about buying a little Bitcoin to dip your toes into digital waters or just curious about how this technology works, staying informed will help you navigate the crypto world more safely and confidently.

So, as you explore the possibilities of cryptocurrencies, remember that like any financial decision, knowledge is power. The more you know, the better prepared you'll be to make smart, informed choices about whether and how to participate in this digital finance revolution.

6.3 Mobile Payments: The Future of Transactions

So, let's talk about mobile payments—a tech trend that's changing the way we think about money faster than you can say "cha-ching!" Gone are the days of fumbling through your pockets for loose change or writing checks (yes, those still exist). With just a few taps on your smartphone, you can pay for almost anything. Services like Apple Pay, Google Wallet, and Venmo are leading the charge, turning your phone into a virtual wallet. But what exactly are mobile payments, and why are they becoming as common as snapping a selfie?

Mobile payments are exactly what they sound like—payments made through your mobile device. Instead of using cash, checks, or physical credit cards, you just use an app on your phone to pay. For instance, with Apple Pay, you can wave your iPhone over a payment terminal, and voila, your payment is made. Google Wallet works similarly but is available on Android devices. Then there's Venmo, which is super popular among teens for splitting dinner bills or paying back friends for movie tickets. It's like sending a text message, but instead of emojis, you're sending cash.

One of the biggest perks of mobile payments is sheer convenience. Picture this: you're wearing your snazziest jeans with those ridiculously small pockets that can barely fit a lip balm, let alone a wallet. With mobile payments, no problem—your phone's already in your hand anyway, right? Plus, it's super quick. No more digging for your wallet, finding the right card, and waiting for change. Just tap and go. It simplifies everything, which is pretty much what we all want, isn't it?

But it's not just about ease. Mobile payments can also be kinder to your wallet. Many apps offer rewards, discounts, or even cashback when you pay with your phone. It's like being paid to be tech-savvy, which, let's be honest, is pretty sweet. And let's not forget the cool factor. Paying with your phone definitely earns you tech-savvy points among friends.

Now, let's talk about security, because let's face it, the internet can be a wild place. Mobile payment systems come packed with advanced security features that make them safer than many traditional payment methods. Tokenization, for example, is a fancy term for a simple concept: it turns your real card number into a random set of numbers (a token) during the transaction, so your actual card details aren't shared with the merchant and can't be stolen. Then there's biometric authentication—think fingerprint scans or facial recognition, which adds an extra layer of security because let's face it, there's only one you.

Setting up mobile payments is usually a breeze. First, choose your app—Apple Pay, Google Wallet, Venmo, or maybe another one that catches your eye. Download it and link it to your bank account or a credit card. This might sound a bit daunting, but it's usually just a matter of entering your card details and maybe a verification step or two to make sure it's really you. Always follow the setup instructions provided by the app, and voila, you're ready to make your first mobile payment.

Whether you're buying a hot dog at a stand, splitting the bill at a restaurant, or just sending some cash to a friend, mobile payments can make it faster, easier, and more secure. With your smartphone already an essential part of your daily life, why not turn it into your wallet too? It's all about making your life a little simpler, one tap at a time. So, next time you're about to make a payment, why not pull out your phone and give it a tap? Welcome to the future of transactions, where your money moves at the speed of your lifestyle.

6.4 Online Security: Keeping Your Financial Data Safe

Imagine the internet as a bustling city—it's got its flashy malls and cozy spots, but it also has some sketchy alleys where you wouldn't want to wander. That's pretty much why online security is a big deal, especially when you're dealing with money. Whether you're shopping, banking, or trading digital coins, keeping your financial data secure is like locking your car in a parking lot—you don't want to come back and find it broken into. So, as the digital 
landscape evolves, staying savvy about online security is more crucial than ever. Let's unpack some of the common threats and arm you with strategies to shield your digital life.

Phishing, malware, and identity theft are the main baddies in the world of online threats, and they're all about deception and theft. Phishing is like those spammy emails or messages that trick you into giving away personal info by pretending to be legit—think of a fake email from your bank asking for your password. Then there's malware, which is basically software designed to harm or exploit any programmable device, service, or network. Malware sneaks in through shady downloads or infected links and can spy on your online activity or steal data. Identity theft? It's the grand heist—it happens when someone steals your personal information to commit fraud, like opening credit accounts in your name, which can mess up your financial health big time.

So, how do you fight off these online villains? First, get serious about your passwords. They're like the keys to your online kingdom. Use strong, unique passwords for different accounts. If 'password123' is your go-to, you might as well leave your digital door wide open. Mix it up with numbers, symbols, and both upper and lower case letters. Consider using a password manager to keep track of all your passwords—it's safer than jotting them down on a sticky note.

Next up, two-factor authentication (2FA) is your cybersecurity buddy. It adds an extra layer of protection by requiring two forms of identification before you can log in. So, even if some sneaky hacker gets your password, they still need the second key to unlock your account. Most social platforms and financial services offer 2FA, so turn it on whenever you can.

Being able to spot a secure website is also key. Always check the URL—secure sites start with 'https' (the extra 's' stands for secure) and often have a little padlock icon next to the URL. This means the site encrypts your data, making it tougher for cyber crooks to snatch your info. So, next time you're about to enter sensitive info like your credit card number, take a second to look for these security signs.

What if, despite all your defenses, you still find yourself a victim of a security breach? First, don't panic. Report the breach to your bank or the service that was compromised. They can help secure your account and track any suspicious activity. Then, change your passwords immediately. If you think your financial information was stolen, consider setting up a fraud alert on your credit reports—it makes it harder for identity thieves to open accounts in your name. Keep an eye on your bank statements and credit reports for any unusual activity. If things look fishy, report them right away.

Staying safe online doesn't have to feel like a spy mission. With these strategies in your toolkit, you can navigate the digital world with confidence, knowing you're taking the right steps to protect your financial data. So, go ahead and explore, shop, and manage your money online—just do it wisely, and keep your digital armor on at all times. Remember, in the vast world of the internet, it's better to be safe than sorry!

6.5 The Influence of Social Media on Financial Decisions

Let's spill the tea on something we all know but might not always admit: social media has a way of making us want things we didn't even know we needed. One minute you're scrolling through your feed, and the next, you're three clicks deep into a shopping cart, thanks to some ultra-slick, super tempting ads. The power of social media to influence our spending habits is real, and it's not just about ads. There's also the subtle (and sometimes not-so-subtle) peer pressure. Pics of your friends sporting the latest fashion trends or that must-have gadget can stir up a serious case of FOMO (Fear of Missing Out), pushing you to buy just to keep up.

But it's not just about what we buy—it's also about whom we trust. Financial advice is everywhere on social media, from TikTok videos on Bitcoin investing to Instagram stories about saving hacks. The tricky part? Not all of it is reliable. Just because someone has a ton of followers doesn't mean they're a financial guru. Some might be sharing advice based on personal experiences that might not apply to everyone, or worse, they could be pushing products or investments that aren't really in your best interest.

Navigating this maze can be tricky, but here's a pro tip: always double-check the info you get. If someone suggests a new savings app or an investment opportunity, take a beat to research it on your own. Look for information from credible sources—think established financial news sites or official financial advisory firms. They might not be as flashy as a viral video, but they're a lot more likely to give you the solid advice you need. And remember, if something sounds too good to be true, like an investment promising big returns with no risk, it probably is.

So, how do you keep from being swept up in the social media spending spree? Setting limits can help—a lot. Start by tracking how much time you spend on social media and what you're looking at. You might realize you're spending more time watching luxury unboxing videos than you thought. From there, consider setting limits on both your screen time and your spending. Many phones now have built-in tools to help you monitor and limit screen time, and you can set budget reminders on your banking apps.

But hey, it's not all doom and gloom. Social media can actually be a fantastic tool for managing your money—if you use it wisely. Follow financial influencers who are known for giving sound advice. Many financial experts share free content that can help you understand everything from budgeting basics to the finer points of investing. Platforms like YouTube or financial blogs can be goldmines for educational content that can help you make smarter financial decisions.

And let's not forget about the positive communities that can be found on social platforms. There are tons of groups and forums where people share their financial journeys, support each other's goals, and offer practical tips. Joining one of these communities can keep you motivated, give you new ideas on how to handle your money, and even help you stay accountable to your financial goals. Just like in real life, finding your tribe online can make a big difference.

In the whirlwind world of likes, shares, and swiping up, keeping a level head about your finances is key. Use social media as a tool to empower, educate, and connect, not just a platform to spend and splurge. With the right approach, those endless scrolls through your feeds can actually turn into a journey of financial growth and savvy saving. So next time you log in, remember: you're in control. Use that power to fuel your financial well-being, not just your next impulse buy.

6.6 Crowdfunding and Peer-to-Peer Lending: New Ways to Access Money

Ever thought about funding your genius idea or finding a way to invest some of your hard-earned cash through the internet? Enter the world of crowdfunding and peer-to-peer (P2P) lending, the cooler, tech-savvy cousins of traditional financing. These platforms aren't just about getting money; they're about connecting people who need money with those who have money to invest. It's kind of like a matchmaking app, but instead of finding a date, you're either scoring funds for your next big project or finding a promising investment.

Crowdfunding is essentially the internet's way of throwing you a financial lifeline. Whether it's launching a new product, recording a music album, or even funding a community project, crowdfunding platforms allow you to pitch your big idea to the world and get people to back you financially. But it's not just about asking for money; depending on the type of crowdfunding, backers can be rewarded in various ways. Donation-based crowdfunding is straightforward – people give money to support a cause they care about without expecting anything in return. Rewards-based crowdfunding offers backers a tangible item or service in return for their funding. Think Kickstarter or Indiegogo, where backing a video game development can snag you an early copy of the game. Then there's equity crowdfunding, where backers get a slice of the ownership pie in the company they invest in, potentially reaping financial rewards if the company takes off.

Participating in crowdfunding requires a solid pitch and a clear understanding of what backers will expect. You'll need to set a funding goal and a timeline, and then work hard to spread the word. Social media is your best friend here, helping you reach a wide audience and drum up support. But remember, transparency is key. Be clear about how the funds will be used and keep your backers updated on the project's progress. It's not just about getting their money, but building trust and maybe turning them into long-term supporters of your ventures.

On the flip side, there's peer-to-peer (P2P) lending, where you can borrow directly from another person without going through a bank. Platforms like Lending Club or Prosper allow people to apply for loans funded by individual investors. As a borrower, you might get lower interest rates than traditional banks offer, and as a lender, you can earn higher returns on your investment than you would from a savings account. It's a win-win—if all goes well. But, as with any investment, there's a risk. Borrowers might default, and lenders could lose their money, which is why these platforms carefully screen applicants and rate them based on risk.

If you're thinking about diving into P2P lending, either as a borrower or a lender, start by choosing a reputable platform. Look for ones that are transparent about their processes and fees and have good reviews for customer service. Understand the terms and conditions, know the interest rates, and get a clear picture of the risk involved. It's also a good idea to start small, especially if you're new to P2P lending, to test the waters before committing more significant amounts of money.

So, whether you're looking to fund your latest invention, invest your savings in a new way, or lend money while earning interest, the digital world offers a plethora of platforms to get started. Crowdfunding and P2P lending are reshaping how money changes hands, making it more accessible, more personalized, and often, more cost-effective. As with any financial decision, do your homework, understand the risks, and start small. With the right approach, these tools can offer exciting opportunities to fund your dreams or grow your investment portfolio.

Financial Savvy Quiz

To check your understanding of digital banking concepts, take this quick quiz! Choose the best answer for each question and find out how digitally savvy you are:

1. **What is digital banking?**

   - A) Banking that only involves cash transactions

   - B) Traditional banking services offered online through apps or websites

   - C) Banking that only takes place in physical bank branches

2. **What is one major benefit of using digital banks over traditional banks?**

   - A) Higher account maintenance fees

   - B) Longer transaction times

   - C) Lower fees due to reduced overhead costs

3. **Which security feature is crucial when choosing a digital**

bank?

- ○ A) Limited customer service hours

- ○ B) Two-factor authentication and encryption

- ○ C) Physical bank branches in multiple locations

4. **What is typically required to set up a digital banking account?**

- ○ A) Only a phone number

- ○ B) Personal information, such as your name, address, and Social Security number, and setting up security features

- ○ C) Visiting a physical branch to fill out forms

5. **What are digital-only banks?**

- ○ A) Banks that have physical branches but also offer online services

- ○ B) Banks that exist entirely online without physical branches

- ○ C) Banks that only handle international transactions

Count your correct answers:

- **5** correct means you're a digital banking whiz!

- **3-4** correct suggests you're well on your way but could use a bit more fine-tuning.

- **2 or below**? Let's boost your digital banking knowledge to ensure you're ready for financial success!

Answers:

1. b) Traditional banking services offered online through apps or websites

2. c) Lower fees due to reduced overhead costs

3. b) Two-factor authentication and encryption

4. b) Personal information, such as your name, address, and Social Security number, and setting up security features

5. b) Banks that exist entirely online without physical branches

As we wrap up this chapter on modern money management, remember that finance today is as much about technology as it is about numbers. From digital banking to cryptocurrencies, and now crowdfunding and P2P lending, the digital landscape is redefining what it means to manage, spend, and invest money. Next up, we'll explore how these innovations are part of a larger shift towards a more connected, more automated world of personal finance. Stay tuned, because the future of money is just getting started, and it's full of opportunities for savvy navigators like you.

CHAPTER 7

FINANCIAL PLANNING FOR FUTURE MILESTONES

Ever thought about how planning for college could be like strategizing for an epic boss battle in your favorite video game? You need the right tools, some serious strategy, and maybe a good sidekick or two. But instead of weapons or power-ups, you are arming yourself with money smarts. That's right, let's talk about saving for college—because diving into your college adventure shouldn't mean drowning in debt.

7.1 Saving for College: Options Beyond Student Loans

Exploring Alternatives to Loans

So, you're eyeing that college diploma like it's the ultimate level-up in life—which, let's face it, it certainly can be. But here's the kicker: you don't have to load up on student loans to get there. There are more ways to fund your higher education than just borrowing money and hoping your future self can handle the debt. Let's unpack some wallet-friendly strategies, shall we? 

First up, we've got 529 plans—these are savings plans that aren't just tax-advantaged, they're like financial growth potions for your college fund. You or your family can put money in, and it grows tax-free as long as you use it for legit educational expenses. Think tuition, books, and even some room and board costs. Plus, some states give you a tax break just for making contributions. It's like getting a high score in saving!

Then, there's the part-time job grind. Whether it's flipping burgers, tutoring, or something cool and techy, earning money now means you borrow less later. And let's not overlook paid internships. They're like the secret levels that unlock valuable work experience while padding your bank account. Both options beef up your resume *and* your savings, giving you a double win.

Benefits of Starting Early

Now, let's talk about timing. Starting early isn't just about being the early bird who gets the worm; it's about giving your money as much time as possible to grow. Thanks to our buddy compound interest, every dollar you stash away now can multiply by the time you're ready for college. It's like planting a tree—the sooner you do it, the bigger it'll be when you need its shade. Or in this case, its cash.

Plus, the earlier you start, the less you have to save each month, which means more money for, you know, life. Starting a savings plan in your freshman year versus your senior year can be the difference between a chill movie night and frantically shaking out couch cushions for spare change.

Family Contributions

Let's not forget the role your squad—aka your family—can play in this quest. They can contribute to your 529 plan or help set up a trust fund. Some might even match your savings dollar for dollar, turning your money into mega money. It's like having team members in a co-op game boosting your stats.

Case Studies

Consider Jenna, who used a combination of a part-time job, scholarships, and a 529 plan contributed to by her relatives to fund her college education. She graduated with only a fraction of the debt her peers had, which is pretty much like finishing a game on expert mode and making it look easy.

Or take Marco, who opted for a paid internship that not only covered his tuition but also led to a full-time job offer post-graduation. Talk about a power move! These real-life success stories show that with the right strategies and a bit of hustle, you can make your college dreams come true without the nightmare of overwhelming debt.

So, as you plot your path to college, remember that loans are not the only way to get there. With some smart saving, timely planning, and maybe a little help from your family, you can hit the books without getting hit by debt. Start now, and you'll thank yourself later—big time.

7.2 Buying Your First Car: Costs and Considerations

So, you're ready to hit the road in your own ride? Getting your first car is like leveling up in real life—it's a mix of freedom and responsibility, wrapped in that new (or new-to-you) car smell. But before you start dreaming of road trips and blasting your playlist through the car speakers, let's talk brass tacks—specifically, the total cost of owning a car. It's not just about the sticker price; there are a bunch of other costs that can sneak up on you faster than a speed bump.

First off, there's the purchase price of the car, which is the big chunk of change you pay upfront or finance over time. But the spending doesn't stop there. You've also got to consider the insurance costs, which can be a real wallet-drainer, especially for younger drivers (who are considered "risky"—go figure). Then there's maintenance—because every car, just like your favorite gaming console, needs a tune-up now and then to keep running smoothly. This includes regular oil changes, tire rotations, and the occasional repair (because sometimes life throws you a flat tire). And we can't forget about fuel costs—unless you're going electric, in which case, swap this for charging costs.

Choosing the right car is like picking the right character in a game—you need one that fits your style and your budget. If you're on a budget, used cars can be great. They're usually cheaper, and the bulk of their depreciation has already occurred, which is a plus. But, like buying an old gaming console, you might run into more repairs down the line. New cars, on the other hand, come with that fresh-off-the-lot shine, generally fewer immediate repair needs, and usually some solid warranties. But, they can depreciate faster than you can say "zero to sixty," meaning they lose value quickly.

Now, about financing your shiny new (or new-to-you) wheels. You've got a few options here. Bank loans are a go-to for many because you can shop around for the best interest rates and terms. Just make sure you understand the fine print, like if there are penalties for paying off the loan early. Dealership financing is another route, and sometimes they offer really low interest rates to reel you in. Just be warned, they're not always the cheapest option in the long run, so do your math. And then there's paying in cash—if you can swing it, it's straightforward and interest-free. You pay upfront, and the car is yours, no monthly payments or interest accruing.

Finally, let's talk negotiation tactics, because paying the sticker price is like starting a game at a disadvantage. Research is your best friend here. Know the fair market value of the car you want, and don't be afraid to haggle a bit. Dealers often have a bit of wiggle room on price, especially if you're there at the end of the month trying to make their sales quotas. Also, always be prepared to walk away. Sometimes the best way to get a better deal is to show you're not afraid to leave without the car. It's like playing hard to get, but with horsepower and finance terms.

So, as you gear up to make one of your first major purchases, remember, a car is not just a way to get from point A to point B—it's a long-term investment that needs careful consideration. Think about all the costs, choose a car that fits your life and your budget, explore your financing options, and don't shy away from negotiating. With the right strategy, you can make sure your first car is a sweet ride without taking your bank account off-road.

7.3 Travel on a Budget: Planning and Saving for Trips

Ever dreamt of exploring distant lands or maybe just zipping away for a weekend beach blast? Whatever your travel fantasy, the reality of costs can sometimes bring you crashing back down to earth. But fear not, fellow globe-trotter, because traveling on a budget doesn't mean skimping on the fun. It's all about smart planning and savvy saving techniques that keep your wallet happy while you rack up those Insta-worthy moments.

Let's start with setting a travel budget, which is kind of like planning your expenses for a big boss battle—you need strategy and foresight. Begin by outlining major expenses like transportation—this could be plane tickets, bus fares, or gas money if you're road-tripping. Next, tackle accommodation costs; from hostels to hotels, prices can vary wildly, so consider what fits your budget and comfort level. Don't forget to factor in daily expenses like food  (street eats or fancy feasts?), activities (museum fees, nightlife), and a little extra for those spontaneous adventures or souvenir shopping. The key here is to overestimate rather than underestimate. It's better to end up with extra cash than to run short in a foreign place.

Now onto the saving part, which, let's be honest, can sometimes feel like a grind. However, setting up a dedicated travel fund can make this a lot less painful. Think of it as your personal travel piggy bank. Whether it's a separate savings account or a money jar in your room, the point is to consistently add to it. Small amounts can snowball over time, especially if you get into the habit of depositing a bit of cash regularly. Apps can also be a game-changer here. Apps like Digit analyze your spending and automatically transfer small amounts to savings, perfect for when you're trying to save without overthinking it.

Traveling cost-effectively is another gem in your budget travel arsenal. One pro tip is to travel during off-peak seasons. Not only are flights and accommodations often cheaper, but you also avoid the tourist rush. Using student discounts can save you a bundle too, so keep that student ID handy. For accommodations, why not ditch expensive hotels and go for hostels, or use platforms like Airbnb to snag cool places at a fraction of the price? And remember, street food isn't just budget-friendly; it's also a way to dive into the local cuisine. Plus, who doesn't love a good food truck rally?

When it comes to planning and booking, think of it as the pre-game prep. Comparing prices online is a must—sites like Skyscanner or Google Flights can help you snag the best deals on airfare, while Booking.com or Hostelworld are go-tos for cheap stays. Always read reviews before you book; they can be a treasure trove of info on what to expect and help you avoid those "I wish I knew" moments. And be sure to understand the cancellation policies; flexible booking options can be a lifesaver if your plans change unexpectedly.

Armed with a solid travel budget, effective savings strategies, cost-effective travel tips, and smart booking practices, you're all set to embark on your next adventure without breaking the bank. So, pack your bags, your budget, and perhaps a handy travel guide, because the world awaits, and now you know how to conquer it wallet-first!

7.4 Financial Aid and Scholarships: Navigating the Maze

Imagine you're gearing up for a giant maze—only this one's filled with paperwork instead of hedges, and at the end, instead of just feeling victorious, you get money to help pay for college. Welcome to the world of financial aid and scholarships! Let's be real, figuring out financial aid can be as confusing as trying to understand the plot in a Christopher Nolan movie. But fear not! With the right info and strategies, you can navigate this maze like a pro.

First things first, let's break down the types of financial aid out there. You've got grants, which are awesome because they're essentially free money. These don't have to be repaid (talk about a sweet deal!). They're often based on financial need, so they're like a financial high-five to students who need that extra bit of support. Then there are scholarships, which are like the golden tickets of college funding. They can be based on all sorts of things—grades, talents, community service, you name it. And like grants, you don't have to repay them. Lastly, there's work-study, which allows you to work part-time while studying (hence the name). This not only pads your wallet but also gives you some solid work experience.

Now, hunting for scholarships can seem daunting—like trying to find a needle in a digital haystack. But with the right tools, you can pinpoint opportunities that feel like they're tailor-made for you. Start with online databases; they're like the search engines of the scholarship world. Websites like Fastweb, Scholarships.com, or the U.S. Department of Labor's free scholarship search tool can help you filter through thousands of options based on your background, interests, and academic aspirations. Also, don't ignore the resources your high school might offer. Guidance counselors often have the inside scoop on local scholarships that might not be on your radar yet. And remember your community organizations, local businesses, and religious institutions—they often have scholarships that get less attention, boosting your chances of landing them.

Crafting applications for scholarships or financial aid is like assembling your best highlight reel. It's not just about boasting academic achievements; it's about storytelling. Whether it's an essay or a personal statement, use this space to paint a picture of who you are beyond your grades. Share your challenges, your triumphs, and what makes you unique. And get your ducks in a row with your financial documentation. Stuff like tax returns, pay stubs, or proof of income can be required. Keeping these documents organized will save you a headache when you're trying to meet those application deadlines.

Avoiding Scams

Here's the kicker—scams. Just when you thought navigating financial aid couldn't get more thrilling, in come the villains. Beware of scholarship offers that ask for payment to apply, or guarantee winnings; they're likely as fake as a three-dollar bill. Remember, if it sounds too good to be true, it probably is. Keep an eye out for unsolicited offers, especially those that ask for personal financial information. These can be phishing attempts looking to reel in your data. Stick to reputable sources and websites when searching for scholarships and never, I repeat, never pay to apply for a scholarship. Real scholarships are about giving money, not taking it.

Navigating the financial aid and scholarship scene doesn't have to feel like a trek through quicksand. With the right knowledge and tools, you can secure the funding you need to support your college journey—minus the debt. So put on your explorer hat, arm yourself with information, and start tackling that maze. Your future self, chilling on campus with the financial wiggle room to actually enjoy college life, will thank you.

7.5 Renting vs. Owning: What Teens Should Know About Housing

So, you're thinking about diving into the big, wide world of housing, huh? Whether it's snagging your first apartment or dreaming of a place you can truly call your own, navigating the housing market is like leveling up in adulting. Let's get real about the pros and cons of renting versus owning. It's a big decision, kind of like choosing between two epic quests, each with its own set of challenges and rewards.

Renting, for starters, is like joining a guild in a game—you're not the leader, but you get a lot of flexibility. You can move around without the hassle of selling a house, which is perfect if you're all about that nomad life or just not ready to plant roots yet. Plus, maintenance headaches? Not your problem. That leaky faucet or the dying fridge is the landlord's quest to handle, not yours. But here's the flip side: you're basically paying for a temporary space. Your monthly rent doesn't build equity or lead to ownership, and sometimes, you might have to deal with rules that limit how you decorate or use your space.

Now, owning a home? That's like building your own castle. It's a place to call your own, and every mortgage payment is like investing in your personal kingdom. Plus, you get the freedom to customize your lair however you want—paint, renovations, epic movie room? Go for it. And financially, owning a home can be a smart move in the long run. If the value of your home increases, so does your investment. But owning also means dealing with all the upkeep, taxes, and mortgage responsibilities. It's a bigger upfront commitment, both in money and responsibilities.

If you're leaning towards renting for the first time, here are some golden nuggets of advice. Understanding your lease agreement is like reading the rules before playing a new game. It outlines what you can and can't do, what your landlord expects, and what you're responsible for as a tenant. Pay close attention to the terms about the security deposit, pet policies, and how to get your full deposit back when you move out. And those rights? They're your in-game power-ups. Know them well to prevent any potential boss battles with a landlord. For instance, you have the right to a safe and habitable living environment, and your landlord should handle repairs in a timely manner.

Path to Homeownership:

Dreaming of swapping your rent receipts for home keys? First, you've got to stack your coins—aka, saving for a down payment. This usually means setting aside 20% of the home's purchase price, which, let's be honest, can feel like hoarding gold for a massive in-game purchase. But here's a pro tip: start small and stay consistent. Even a small amount saved regularly can grow big over time.

Building credit is another crucial step and this is where your credit score comes into play. Think of your credit score as your character's reputation level. The better your reputation, the more trust you earn, which in this realm, translates to better mortgage terms and interest rates. Pay bills on time, keep your debts low, and monitor your credit score regularly to ensure there are no errors pulling down your stats.

Understanding mortgages can feel like decoding ancient runes, but it's not as complex once you break it down. A mortgage is basically a loan for buying property, and it comes with different terms and rates. Fixed-rate mortgages keep the same interest rate over the life of the loan, making budgeting easier. Adjustable-rate mortgages might start lower, but the rate changes based on market conditions, which can be a bit of a gamble.

Real Estate Basics:

Entering the realm of real estate is like stepping into a new game level with its own set of vocab. Terms like "appraisal" (evaluating a property's value), "closing costs" (fees paid at the end of a real estate transaction), and "equity" (the difference between the property's value and what you owe on the mortgage) are part of the lingo. Getting to know these terms is like mastering the basic controls before you start playing in earnest.

Whether you choose to rent or own, each path offers unique advantages and challenges. Like choosing paths in a game, each choice leads to different outcomes and experiences. So consider your lifestyle preferences, financial situation, and long-term goals when making your decision. And remember, whether you're signing a lease or closing on a house, you're leveling up in your personal finance adventure.

7.6 Insurance Basics: Protecting Your Financial Future

Think of insurance as your financial safety net—kind of like the protective gear you'd wear when trying out some extreme sports. It's not the most thrilling part of adulting, but it's crucial for avoiding major financial face-plants. Whether it's a fender bender in your new car, a stolen laptop, or an unexpected trip to the hospital, insurance can be the superhero that saves the day (and your bank account). Let's get into the nuts and bolts of picking the right insurance, managing costs, and navigating the claims process without losing your mind.

First up, why is insurance a must-have in your financial toolkit? Well, life loves throwing curveballs, and insurance is your bat, ready to knock those surprises out of the park. There are several types you might need: health insurance, because let's face it, nobody is invincible; auto insurance, which is actually mandatory if you're driving; and renter's (or homeowners) insurance, which covers your stuff in case your home becomes the set of a disaster movie. Each type of insurance is designed to handle specific risks, ensuring that an accident or emergency doesn't derail your financial future.

Choosing the right insurance starts with assessing your needs. It's like picking a character in a video game—you want the one whose skills match the challenge ahead. Are you a commuter or a homebody? This affects whether comprehensive auto insurance or basic coverage is better for you. Do you live in a dorm or off-campus apartment? That determines if you need renter's insurance. Once you've figured out what you need, it's time to compare providers. Look at their coverage options, premiums (that's the price you pay, usually monthly), customer service ratings, and reviews. It's a bit like online shopping, but instead of looking for the best sneakers, you're hunting for the best protection at the right price.

Managing insurance costs is next. Think of this as the budgeting level of your insurance game. Premiums can eat up a chunk of your cash if you're not careful, but there are ways to keep costs down. Shopping around is a no-brainer—different companies can offer the same coverage at wildly different prices. Consider bundling policies; many companies will give you a discount if you get multiple types of insurance with them. And look at raising your deductibles, which are what you pay out of pocket before your insurance kicks in. Higher deductibles can significantly lower your premiums. Just make sure you have enough saved to cover the deductible if you need to.

Now, let's talk about handling claims, because eventually, you might need to use your insurance. First, know what your policy covers and what it doesn't. Keep all relevant documents, like your insurance policy and receipts for valuables, in a safe place (and maybe a digital backup, too). If you need to file a claim, document everything. For a car accident, take photos at the scene. For health issues, keep track of medical visits and bills. Contact your insurance provider as soon as possible, and follow their steps for filing a claim. Be thorough but patient—sometimes, getting a claim processed is a marathon, not a sprint.

Navigating the world of insurance isn't as hard as it looks once you understand the basics. With the right coverage, you're not just protecting your stuff—you're protecting your peace of mind. Plus, understanding insurance now sets you up with the know-how to handle bigger investments in the future, like buying a home or starting a business. So take the time to get your insurance game on point, and you'll be ready for whatever life throws your way.

Financial Savvy Quiz

To check your understanding of saving for college beyond student loans, take this quick quiz! Choose the best answer for each question and see how prepared you are for funding your education:

1. What is a major benefit of a 529 plan?

   ○ A) It grows tax-free when used for educational expenses

   ○ B) It can be used for any type of expense

   ○ C) It requires no initial investment

2. How can a part-time job benefit you while in college?

   ○ A) It offers free tuition

   ○ B) It provides valuable work experience and reduces the need for loans

   ○ C) It guarantees a job after graduation

3. Why is it beneficial to start saving for college early?

- ○ A) You can avoid applying for scholarships

- ○ B) It eliminates the need for financial aid

- ○ C) It reduces the amount you need to save each month due to compound interest

4. How can family members contribute to your college savings?

- ○ A) By co-signing on student loans

- ○ B) By contributing to your 529 plan or setting up a trust fund

- ○ C) By paying for your daily expenses

5. What is a potential advantage of paid internships?

- ○ A) They cover tuition and can lead to job offers after graduation

- ○ B) They provide free housing

- ○ C) They allow you to skip classes

Count your correct answers:

- 5 correct means you're a college savings expert!

- 3-4 correct suggests you're on the right track but could use a bit more planning.

- 2 or below? Let's enhance your knowledge on saving for college to ensure you're ready for financial success!

Answers:

1. a) It grows tax-free when used for educational expenses

2. b) It provides valuable work experience and reduces the need for loans

3. c) It reduces the amount you need to save each month due to compound interest

4. b) By contributing to your 529 plan or setting up a trust fund

5. a) They cover tuition and can lead to job offers after graduation

As we wrap up this chapter on navigating major financial milestones, from college savings plans to insurance basics, remember that each step you take builds on the last. Whether you're saving for college, buying your first car, planning a budget-friendly trip, or picking out your first insurance policy, each decision is a building block towards a secure and prosperous future. Next up, we'll dive into some advanced personal finance strategies that can really amp up your money management game. Stay tuned for more tools and tips to keep leveling up your financial prowess.

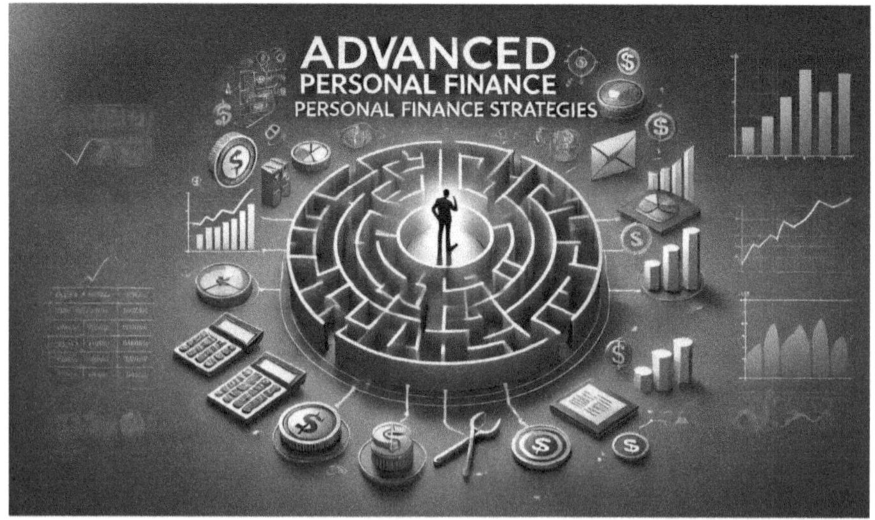

CHAPTER 8

ADVANCED PERSONAL FINANCE STRATEGIES

Imagine you've just aced the ultimate boss battle in your favorite game, but instead of game points, you're scoring real cash. That's kind of what diving into the world of salary negotiations feels like. Whether you're gearing up for your first job or aiming for a raise, understanding the ins and outs of negotiating your salary can feel like leveling up in real life. So, let's gear up, power up your confidence, and get you ready to negotiate like a pro!

8.1 Negotiating Salaries: Tactics for Your First Job or Raise

Understanding the Negotiation Process

The first thing you need to know about salary negotiation is that it's not a showdown, but more like a dance. It's about finding a rhythm that works for both you and your employer. First off, why is it so important? Well, starting with the right salary sets the tone for your earnings now and in the future because most of your raises will be a percentage of what you currently earn. So, starting higher can snowball into much more over your career.

Now, the cornerstone of any good negotiation is research. Before you even start talking numbers, you need to know what the going rate is for your role in your industry and your location. Websites like Glassdoor, PayScale, and LinkedIn Salary can be your treasure maps. They give you the lay of the land on what others in your field are earning. Remember, knowledge is power—especially when it's about dollars and cents!

Preparation Strategies

Once you've armed yourself with knowledge, it's time to look inward. Reflect on your accomplishments. Maybe you aced a relevant project, or you have skills that are in high demand. Create a list of your achievements and think about how they align with the needs of the job. This list is your arsenal during negotiations. It shows why you deserve not just the base salary but potentially more. Think of it as your highlight reel—every point is a reason for why they should pay you what you're asking.

Preparation doesn't stop there. Practice makes perfect, right? Try role-playing the negotiation with a friend or family member, preferably someone who's been through a few negotiations themselves. They can throw different scenarios at you, giving you a chance to respond and adapt your strategy. This practice can make the actual conversation feel less intimidating and more like a dialogue you're ready to ace.

Negotiation Dos and Don'ts

Alright, game time! Here are some quick dos and don'ts in the negotiation arena:

- Do be clear and confident: State your case and back it up with your research and accomplishments.

- Do express gratitude: Start by thanking your potential employer for the opportunity. It sets a positive tone and shows you're not just about the money.

- Don't make demands: This is a discussion, not a demand letter. Keep the tone conversational and cooperative.

- Don't use ultimatums: Unless you're genuinely willing to walk away, avoid painting yourself into a corner with ultimatums. They can backfire and close down negotiations before they truly start.

Scenario-Based Role Play:

Let's dive into a role-play scenario you might find relatable. Imagine you're applying for a summer job at a local computer shop, and the initial offer is $10 an hour. However, your research and discussions with friends who work in similar shops indicate that the average rate is closer to $12 an hour. Here's how you could approach the negotiation:

You: "Thank you so much for the job offer! I'm really looking forward to the opportunity to work here, especially since I'm passionate about technology and excited to help customers with their computer needs. I've talked to a few friends and done a bit of research, and I found that the going rate for similar positions in our area is usually around $12 an hour. Considering my skills with computer repairs and customer service from my previous volunteering, I think $12 an hour would be a fair rate that reflects the value I can bring to your team."

This approach shows you're informed, you appreciate the offer, and you're also aware of your value. Plus, it opens the door for further discussion.

Navigating salary negotiations can be one of your first real tests in the world of personal finance. But with the right preparation and mindset, you can turn it into a constructive conversation that sets the stage for your financial future. Remember, it's not just about getting what you want; it's about creating an agreement that benefits both you and your employer. Now, go forth and negotiate like the savvy financial gamer you are—power-ups ready!

8.2 Investing in Real Estate: Basics for Young Investors

So, you're thinking about stepping into the real estate game? That's like leveling up from lemonade stands to owning a piece of the block! Real estate isn't just for the old and wealthy; it's a field bursting with opportunities, even for younger folks. Let's break down the basics, from what kind of properties are out there to how you can start investing without needing a billionaire's budget.

First things first: real estate investment isn't just buying homes. It's about making strategic decisions on various types of properties. You've got residential properties, which are all about homes and apartments. Then there are commercial properties, which can be anything from a tiny boutique to a sprawling office complex. And let's not forget about industrial spaces like warehouses, or even raw land, which is just what it sounds like – undeveloped land waiting for someone with a vision to turn it into something profitable.

Now, diving into real estate means getting comfy with market analysis. This is where you play detective, scoping out the area where you're thinking of investing. What's the neighborhood like? Are businesses booming? Are people moving in or out? This kind of intel can tell you whether a property's value might shoot up or plummet down. It's all about location, location, location – and a bit of future-gazing to boot. For instance, a sleepy town with a new college or tech hub nearby could mean properties there are about to go up in value.

When it comes to strategies, there's more than one way to invest. You could go the traditional route of buying a property and either living in it or renting it out. Or you could get into flipping houses, where you buy a fixer-upper, jazz it up, and sell it for a profit. Then there's wholesaling, which involves securing a contract on a property and then selling the contract to another investor without ever having to handle a paintbrush or hammer.

Benefits and Risks

Like any good game, real estate has its power-ups and pitfalls. On the bright side, properties can generate rental income and might appreciate over time, giving you a nice profit if you decide to sell. Real estate can also be a hedge against inflation because as living costs go up, so can rent and property values. Plus, owning real estate can offer some tax benefits, like deductions for mortgage interest, property taxes, and costs involved in buying, managing, and selling the property.

However, let's not sugarcoat it – there are risks too. The market can be fickle, with property values swinging based on economic conditions, interest rates, and even changes in neighborhood popularity. Properties also come with ongoing costs, like maintenance, taxes, and insurance, not to mention the headache potential from dealing with tenants or unexpected repairs. And unlike stocks or bonds, you can't just sell off part of a property to raise a little cash – it's all or nothing.

Getting Started

So, how do you jump into real estate without a mountain of cash? One word: REITs, or Real Estate Investment Trusts. These are companies that own or finance income-producing real estate across various sectors. Think of REITs as mutual funds for real estate. You can buy shares of a REIT just like stocks, which means you can invest in real estate for the cost of a few shares. REITs are required by law to distribute most of their taxable income to shareholders, so they can also provide a steady income stream.

Another option is to look into real estate partnerships, where you team up with other investors to buy property. This can be a great way to pool resources and share the risks and rewards. Just make sure you have a clear agreement and understand the terms before you dive in, as partnerships can get tricky if everyone's not on the same page.

Case Studies

Let's look at some real-life young investors who've made their mark in the real estate world. Take Sarah, for example. She started by investing in a small REIT during college. By the time she graduated, her shares had grown enough to help her put a down payment on a small condo. She lived there for a few years, then rented it out after moving for a job. The rental income has been paying her mortgage, and the property's value has nearly doubled.

Then there's Carlos, who teamed up with friends to buy a multi-unit fixer-upper. They renovated the units one by one and rented them out, using the rental income to finance further renovations. Two years later, they sold the property for a tidy profit, which they reinvested in larger properties.

These stories show that with the right strategy, a bit of risk management, and some elbow grease, real estate investing can be accessible and profitable, even for younger investors. Whether you're looking to buy a small share in a REIT or get hands-on with property management, the real estate market is a playground of opportunities waiting for you to make your mark. So, why not start exploring your options? Who knows, the next real estate success story could be yours!

8.3 Advanced Budgeting: Balancing Multiple Financial Goals

So, you've got big dreams, right? Maybe you're saving up for a killer road trip, aiming to start your own side hustle, or even squirreling away funds for college. That's a lot of financial balls to keep in the air! Crafting a budget that juggles multiple goals without dropping any isn't just smart; it's crucial. Let's break down how you can create a multi-goal budget that works as hard as you do.

First off, think of your budget as your personal financial dashboard. It shows you what's coming in, what's going out, and where you need to steer next. To manage multiple goals, you need a clear visual of all your financial targets in one place. Start by listing each goal along with the amount you need and your deadline to hit that target. This could look something like: "$500 for summer music festival by June," "$2000 for laptop upgrade by September," and so on.

Now, here comes the fun part—prioritization. Not all financial goals carry the same weight. Some might be essential (like saving for textbooks), while others might be more flexible (like upgrading your gaming setup). Sort your goals into categories based on urgency and importance. A cool trick is to use color-coding or tagging systems in a budgeting app to keep everything straight. Apps like Mint or YNAB (You Need a Budget) are great for this because they let you create specific categories and set goals for each, tracking your progress in real-time.

But what about when life throws a curveball, and your financial situation shifts? Maybe you score a great summer job or, on the flip side, have unexpected expenses like a phone repair. That's why regularly reviewing and adjusting your budget is crucial. Set a monthly 'budget date' with yourself to sit down and review your financials. Check how you're tracking against your goals and adjust your allocations if needed. Maybe you're way ahead on saving for that new laptop and can afford to redirect some funds to your road trip fund. Or perhaps you need to tighten up on some leisure spending to keep on track for your bigger goals.

Using advanced tools and apps can seriously streamline this process. Many budgeting apps offer features that allow you to view your progress on various goals and adjust your contributions with just a few taps. They can also send you alerts if you're falling behind, so you can correct your course quickly. Plus, seeing your progress visually can be a huge motivational boost. Nothing like watching those progress bars get closer to full to make you feel like you're winning at the finance game!

Balancing multiple financial goals might seem like a juggling act, but with the right tools and a solid plan, you can keep all your balls in the air. By setting clear priorities, regularly reviewing your budget, and leveraging technology to keep you on track, you're not just managing your money; you're mastering it. So, keep your eyes on your financial goals, adjust as you go, and remember, every step you take is moving you closer to making those dreams a reality.

8.4 Legal Financial Products: Understanding Contracts and Agreements

Hey, so here's the scoop on something super important but often as overlooked as the 'terms and conditions' checkbox on a new app download—understanding legal financial documents. Whether it's a loan agreement, a lease for your first apartment, or an insurance policy, these documents are more than just boring legal jargon; they're contracts that can impact your financial health and future. So let's decode these cryptic texts and make sure you're not accidentally signing up for something that could backfire.

First off, let's tackle common financial contracts and agreements you might stumble upon. Loan agreements are pretty straightforward—they outline the terms under which money is borrowed and must be repaid, often with interest. These are super common if you're taking out student loans or financing a car. Next up are leases, which you'll definitely run into if you're renting a place. Leases lay out the dos and don'ts of your rental situation, how much you need to cough up each month, and what happens if you decide to move out early. Then, there's insurance policies. These are agreements that promise you compensation for specific potential future losses in exchange for a periodic payment, or premium. It could be for your car, your health, or even your apartment's renter's insurance.

Now, reading and understanding these documents can be as tricky as trying to understand your phone bill's fine print. The key here is not to rush. Take your time to go through each section. Look out for key terms like 'interest rate,' 'penalty for late payment,' and 'renewal terms.' These aren't just formalities; they're conditions you're agreeing to uphold. A good strategy is to highlight anything you don't understand or that seems out of place. This could be clauses about additional fees or rules about what you can and cannot do in a rental property, such as pet policies or customization rules.

Getting why it's crucial not to skip the fine print yet? Here's another reason: sometimes companies include clauses that might not be in your favor, like mandatory arbitration or clauses that prevent you from joining class action lawsuits. These might not seem like a big deal now, but they can limit your options if things go south. Always remember, the devil is in the details. Understanding every part of your contract means you won't get caught off-guard by something you agreed to without realizing.

Speaking of details, there are times when it's wise to get some backup—in the form of legal advice. Especially if you're about to sign something significant, like a hefty loan agreement or a long-term lease. Lawyers can be lifesavers here, helping you navigate complex language and ensuring that your rights are protected. For instance, if you're unsure about the implications of a particular clause in a lease or an insurance policy, a quick consultation with a legal expert can clarify whether it's standard stuff or something to negotiate out of.

Let's look at a couple of real-world scenarios where not paying attention to the fine print led to headaches. Think about Jessica, a college student who signed up for a credit card with what seemed like great terms. She missed the part about the interest rate skyrocketing after the first year. When her interest rate jumped from 5% to 20%, her debt started piling up faster than she could handle. Or consider Mike, who rushed through signing his apartment lease and didn't notice a 'no early termination' clause. When he got a job offer in another city and had to move, he was stuck paying rent for several months on an apartment he wasn't living in.

Both of these headaches could have been avoided with a more careful review and understanding of their contracts. By taking the time to understand every agreement and seeking legal advice when necessary, you can protect yourself from similar pitfalls. Remember, every contract or agreement is more than just paper; it's a commitment that can affect your financial future. So, treat them with the seriousness they deserve, and you'll be way ahead of most people who glance and sign. After all, in the world of personal finance, being informed isn't just useful; it's your best defense.

8.5 Financial Independence: The Path to Early Retirement

Imagine hitting snooze on your alarm clock for the last time, not because it's the weekend, but because you're financially independent and can choose how to spend every day. That's the ultimate dream, right? Financial independence and early retirement (FIRE) aren't just buzzwords; they're achievable goals that can allow you to live life on your terms. So, how do you turn this dream into a reality? Let's break it down.

Financial independence means having enough income to cover your living expenses for the rest of your life without having to work full time. Early retirement kicks this up a notch, not just achieving financial independence early but also having the freedom to retire well before the traditional re-tirement age. This might sound like a luxury reserved for the ultra-wealthy, but with the right strategies, it's within reach for a lot of people, including you.

The journey towards financial independence starts with aggressive saving. Think of it as putting your money on a super strict diet. The more you can save and the less you spend, the faster you'll reach your goal. This isn't about pinching pennies or never enjoying a pizza night with friends; it's about making smart choices to boost your savings rate. For instance, opting for a less expensive car or living in a more affordable area can free up a lot of cash that can go straight into your savings.

Next up is investing wisely. Saving alone won't get you to financial inde-pendence; you need your money to grow. Investing in the stock market, real estate, or other assets can help your savings compound over time. It's like planting a tree; it takes time to grow, but eventually, it can provide enough shade to shelter you. The key here is to start early, invest regularly, and maintain a diversified portfolio to manage risks and maximize returns.

Minimizing expenses is another crucial strategy. This goes hand-in-hand with aggressive saving but focuses more on cutting ongoing costs. This could mean anything from reducing utility bills and minimizing eating out to cutting back on subscriptions you don't really need. Every dollar you don't spend is a dollar that can be saved and invested towards your financial independence.

Now, let's talk about the FIRE movement, which stands for Financial Independence, Retire Early. This movement has gained a lot of traction among those who want to ditch the traditional 9-to-5 grind and enjoy life on their own terms. There are several variations of FIRE, each tailored to different lifestyles and goals. Lean FIRE means living on a minimal budget to achieve independence faster, while Fat FIRE involves a more comfort-able lifestyle with a larger budget. Then there's Barista FIRE, where you're mostly financially independent but work part-time, like a barista, to cover some living expenses without dipping into your savings.

Case Studies of Early Retirees

Let's look at some real-life champions of FIRE who have successfully navi-gated their path to early retirement. Take Lucy, for example. She embraced the Lean FIRE approach right out of college, living frugally and saving over 70% of her income. By investing in a mix of stocks and bonds, she was able to retire at 32. Now, she spends her days traveling and volunteering, funding her lifestyle with the passive income from her investments.

Then there's Raj, who went the Fat FIRE route. He chose to live comfortably but below his means during his high-earning years as a software developer. By saving and investing wisely, he built a substantial portfolio that allowed him to retire at 40. Raj now enjoys a relaxed lifestyle, indulging in his passion for photography and teaching coding to kids in his community.

These stories illustrate that financial independence and early retirement aren't just fantasies. They're achievable with the right mix of discipline, smart financial choices, and a bit of creativity in how you manage your money. Whether you're aiming for Lean FIRE, Fat FIRE, or something in between, the freedom to choose how you live your life without financial constraints is a powerful goal. So, why not start plotting your own path to FIRE? With each dollar you save and invest, you're not just securing your future; you're also paving the way for a life where you call the shots. After all, who says you have to wait until your 60s to enjoy retirement? With financial independence, the choice is yours, and the time to start is now.

8.6 Continuing Financial Education: Lifelong Learning Strategies

Hey, so you've got a handle on your budget, you're investing, and maybe you've even dipped your toes into negotiating salaries or real estate. Feels pretty good, right? But here's the thing: the world of finance is like the internet—constantly evolving, endlessly fascinating, and full of cat videos. Okay, maybe not the last part. But just like you can't watch just one cat video, you can't stop learning about finance after setting up a budget. Financial education is a continuous journey, with new things to learn and new tools to master. So, how do you keep your financial knowledge fresh and relevant? Let's dive into some strategies that will keep you sharp and savvy.

First off, why is ongoing financial education so crucial? Well, think of it like updating your phone or computer. If you don't install updates, you miss out on new features, and things might start to glitch. The economy, financial laws, and even financial products are in a constant state of flux, and staying informed helps you adapt and make smarter decisions. Plus, the more you know, the less likely you are to fall for scams or make decisions that could hurt your financial health long-term.

Now, where do you go for this knowledge? You're in luck because there are tons of resources out there. For starters, books are your best friends. And no, they don't have to be those thick, snooze-inducing tomes that double as doorstops. There are plenty of engaging, insightful books on personal finance that are as easy to digest as your favorite novel. "I Will Teach You To Be Rich" by Ramit Sethi, for example, breaks down complex financial concepts into humorous, easy-to-understand advice. Another great read is "Rich Dad Poor Dad" by Robert Kiyosaki, which provides valuable insights through the contrasting financial teachings he received from his father and his best friend's father.

But maybe you're more of an auditory learner? Podcasts are perfect for soaking up info while you're on the go. Tune into shows like "The Dave Ramsey Show" for advice on getting out of debt and managing your money, or "Planet Money" by NPR, which explains economic concepts in a really fun and engaging way. These can turn your commute or downtime into a productive mini-classroom.

And let's not forget about online courses. Websites like Coursera and Udemy offer courses on everything from basic budgeting to advanced investing, often taught by top-notch professionals from around the world. Many of these courses are free or offered at a low cost, making them an accessible option for anyone looking to deepen their financial knowledge.

Incorporating learning into your daily life can be as simple as following financial news sites or blogs that resonate with your interests. Set up a daily or weekly routine to check sites like Bloomberg, CNBC, or even financial subreddits and forums. This not only keeps you updated on financial news but also exposes you to different perspectives and strategies that you might not have considered.

Lastly, staying curious and critical is key. With the flood of information available, it's important to keep your critical thinking hat on. Not all advice will be relevant or beneficial for your specific situation. Learn to evaluate the source of the information, question the motives behind the advice, and cross-reference tips with other trusted sources. This will help you build not just knowledge, but wisdom that you can rely on to make decisions.

By embracing these strategies, you're not just staying informed; you're actively shaping your financial future. Keep feeding your brain with fresh, relevant information, and you'll be amazed at how much more confident and proactive you become in managing your finances. Remember, in the world of personal finance, learning never goes out of style. So keep exploring, asking questions, and expanding your financial understanding. Your future self will thank you.

Financial Savvy Quiz

To check your understanding of financial terms and concepts, take this quick quiz! Choose the correct answer for each question:

1. What is the first step in preparing for a salary negotiation?
   A) Demanding a high salary

B) Researching the going rate for your role in your industry and location
C) Writing a resignation letter

2. Why is starting with the right salary so important?
   A) It sets the tone for future earnings and raises
   B) It impresses your colleagues
   C) It makes your job easier

3. What should you do before the actual salary negotiation conversation?
   A) Ignore your past accomplishments
   B) Reflect on your achievements and how they align with the job's needs
   C) Threaten to leave if you don't get a raise

4. Which of the following is a recommended practice during salary negotiations?
   A) Making demands and ultimatums
   B) Ignoring the employer's perspective
   C) Expressing gratitude and keeping the tone conversational

5. In a role-play scenario, if you find out the average rate for similar positions is higher than the offer you received, how should you approach the negotiation?
   A) "I've done some research and found that the going rate for similar positions in our area is usually around $12 an hour. Considering my skills and experience, I think this would be a fair rate."
   B) "This offer is too low. I deserve more."
   C) "I won't accept anything less than $15 an hour."

Count your correct answers:

- 5 correct means you're a negotiation whiz!

- 3-4 correct suggests you're well on your way but could use a bit more fine-tuning.

- 2 or below? Let's boost your negotiation knowledge to ensure you're ready for financial success!

Answers:

1. b) Researching the going rate for your role in your industry and location

2. a) It sets the tone for future earnings and raises

3. b) Reflect on your achievements and how they align with the job's needs

4. c) Expressing gratitude and keeping the tone conversational

5. a) "I've done some research and found that the going rate for similar positions in our area is usually around $12 an hour. Considering my skills and experience, I think this would be a fair rate."

And that wraps up our deep dive into advanced personal finance strategies! From negotiating paychecks to buying real estate, from mastering complex budgets to understanding the fine print in contracts, we've covered a lot of ground. Each step, each strategy you've learned is a tool in your financial toolkit, ready to help you build a secure, prosperous future. So keep learning, keep planning, and most importantly, keep dreaming big. After all, your financial journey is just beginning, and the possibilities are endless.

CONCLUSION

Hey there, savvy spender and future financial guru! You've just breezed through a whirlwind tour of personal finance, and I hope you're feeling pumped and ready to take on the world—or at least your wallet. From deciphering the mystic arts of budgeting and saving to diving headfirst into the wild waters of investing and managing your dough online, we've covered some serious ground together.

Let's remember that this journey all started with the basics, those building blocks that set you up for all the cool finance tricks you now know. We've journeyed from simple concepts like understanding what APR means, all the way to plotting your path to early retirement and navigating the ever-evolving digital financial landscape.

But why is all this important? Because knowledge is power, my friend! The tools and insights we've explored here arm you with the power to make choices that can lead to a wallet as hefty as your dreams. Starting early—like, right-now early—gives you the magical advantage of compound interest, and trust me, it's a game-changer. It means your money grows while you're busy gaming, sleeping, or conquering the chaos of high school.

And let's get real—money matters are always morphing. New tech, shifting economies, and fresh trends mean you've gotta stay on your toes. But fear not! The core money-smart strategies you've learned here are your trusty sidekicks, ready to adapt right alongside you.

Now, don't just sit there! Get out there and flex those financial muscles. Open that savings account, set up a budgeting app, or chat about your money goals over pizza with someone who's been in the game longer. Experiment with what you've learned—tweak it, twist it, make it work for you. And hey, keep that curiosity alive! The world of finance is as vast as it is thrilling, filled with opportunities to learn more and do better.

Before we part ways, I just want to say thanks. Thanks for joining me on this epic finance adventure. I'm stoked about the smart money moves you're going to make. Remember, I believe in you and your ability to make those big dreams a wallet-sized reality. Start today, keep learning, and keep aiming high. Here's to your incredibly bright, financially savvy future!

So, what are you waiting for? Go make your mark, future mogul!

"Saving money isn't just about being smart; it's about being kind and helping others grow their dreams too." - E.J. Goldwyn

Hey there, financial whiz kid! You've just navigated through the exciting world of personal finance, from saving your first dollar to thinking about investing. I hope you're feeling empowered and ready to shape your financial future. Remember, we started with the basics and built up to some pretty cool money skills!

But why did we go through all this? Because being smart with money isn't just good for you—it's good for everyone around you too. Starting to manage your money wisely at a young age, like right now, gives you a head start. And who knows? You might inspire someone else to start their financial journey because they saw what you could do.

Now, I have a small but powerful way you can help others even more. Most people choose which books to read based on recommendations, so your opinion really matters. Could you help a fellow young saver by leaving a review?

Here's how you can make a big difference without spending a dime or more than a minute:

Please leave a review for this book.

Your review doesn't cost anything and takes just a moment, but it could help someone else discover the magic of managing money. Your words could help:

...another teenager start saving early.
...a young entrepreneur fund their first business.
...a student avoid debt while they study.
...a friend make smart choices with their allowance.
...one more dream of financial freedom come true.

Just scan the QR code below (or click the link on ebook) to leave your review:

[https://www.amazon.com/review/review-your-purchases/?asin=B0D9MX7BZN]

If you're excited about helping another young person learn to manage their money, then you're exactly who this book was written for. Welcome to the club! You're one of us now.

- Your biggest fan, E.J. Goldwyn

GLOSSARY

A

1099 Form: A tax form used to report income from self-employment, interest, dividends, and more. It shows money you earned but weren't employed for, like freelance work.

APR (Annual Percentage Rate): The yearly interest rate charged on borrowed money or earned through an investment, expressed as a percentage.

Appraisal: An expert's estimate of the value of something, like a house, usually needed when buying or selling property.

B

Bonds: Loans you give to companies or the government in return for regular interest payments and the promise to repay the loan on a set date.

Budget: A plan that outlines how you will spend and save your money over a certain period.

C

Certificates of Deposit (CDs): Savings accounts that hold a fixed amount of money for a fixed period, like six months or one year, and typically offer higher interest rates than regular savings accounts.

Checking Account: A bank account used for everyday expenses. It allows you to write checks, use a debit card, and withdraw money easily.

Closing Costs: Fees and expenses you pay when you buy or sell a house, on top of the price of the property itself.

Compound Interest: Interest calculated on both the initial amount of money and the interest that has already been added to it. It helps your money grow faster.

Credit: Borrowing money that you agree to pay back later, often with interest.

Credit Card: A card that lets you borrow money up to a certain limit to buy things. You pay back the borrowed amount later, often with interest.

Credit Score: A number that represents how likely you are to repay borrowed money, based on your credit history.

Credit Utilization: The percentage of your credit limit that you're using. Keeping it low can help your credit score.

Crowdfunding: Raising small amounts of money from a large number of people, typically via the internet, to fund a project or venture.

Cryptocurrency: Digital or virtual money that uses cryptography for security and operates independently of a central bank.

Custodial Account: A financial account set up by an adult for a minor, where the minor owns the money but the adult manages the account.

D

Debit Card: A card that takes money directly from your checking account when you buy something.

Debt (Good Debt vs. Bad Debt): Money you owe. Good debt is used to buy things that can grow in value or generate income, like education or a house. Bad debt is for things that don't add value, like a fancy car or a big-screen TV.

Digital Banking: Managing your bank accounts and financial transactions online through a website or mobile app.

E

Emergency Fund: Money set aside for unexpected expenses, like medical bills or car repairs.

Envelope System: A budgeting method where you divide your cash into envelopes for different spending categories, like food, rent, and entertainment.

Entrepreneur: A person who starts and runs their own business.

ETF's (Exchange-Traded Funds): Investment funds that are traded on stock exchanges, much like stocks. They hold assets like stocks, commodities, or bonds.

Equity: The value of ownership in something, like a house or business, after subtracting any debts owed on it.

F

Financial Independence and Early Retirement (FIRE): A movement aimed at gaining financial independence and retiring early by saving and investing a large portion of your income.

G

Grants: Money given to you that you don't have to pay back, often for education or research.

I

Identity Theft: When someone steals your personal information to commit fraud or other crimes.

Insurance: A contract that helps protect you from financial loss. You pay a premium, and if something bad happens, the insurance company helps cover the costs.

Interest Rates: The cost of borrowing money or the return for investing money, expressed as a percentage.

L

Liquidity: How easily you can convert an asset into cash without losing value.

Loans: Money you borrow that you must pay back with interest over a set period.

M

Malware: Malicious software designed to harm or exploit any programmable device or network.

Mutual Funds: Investment funds that pool money from many people to buy a diversified portfolio of stocks, bonds, or other securities.

P

Peer-to-Peer (P2P): Financial transactions directly between individuals, usually facilitated by a third-party platform.

Phishing: A scam where attackers send fake messages to trick you into giving away personal information like passwords or credit card numbers.

R

Real Estate Investment Trusts (REITs): Companies that own, operate, or finance income-producing real estate. They allow you to invest in real estate without actually buying property.

Return on Investment (ROI): A measure of the profitability of an investment, calculated as a percentage of the original amount invested.

Roth IRA: A retirement savings account where you pay taxes on money going in, but future withdrawals are tax-free.

S

Savings Account: A bank account that earns interest on the money you deposit, helping it grow over time.

Scholarships: Money awarded to you, often for education, that you don't have to pay back, usually based on merit or need.

SMART Goals: Specific, Measurable, Achievable, Relevant, and Time-bound goals that help you plan and achieve your objectives.

Stocks: Shares of ownership in a company that you can buy. Owning stock means you own a piece of that company.

Student Loans: Money borrowed to pay for education, which must be paid back with interest.

T

Tax Deduction: An amount you can subtract from your taxable income, lowering the amount of taxes you owe.

Tax Return: A form you file with the government each year, showing how much money you made and how much tax you owe or get back.

Taxes: Money you pay to the government, which is used to fund public services and projects.

Tokenization: The process of replacing sensitive data, like credit card numbers, with unique symbols (tokens) to protect the data during transactions.

Two-Factor Authentication (2FA): A security process where you need two forms of identification to access your account, making it harder for unauthorized people to get in.

W

W-2 Form: A tax form your employer sends you, showing how much you earned and how much tax was withheld from your paycheck.

W-4 Form: A form you fill out when you start a new job, telling your employer how much tax to withhold from your paycheck.

Work-Study: A program that helps students earn money for education by working part-time jobs.

# #

529 Plans: Education savings plans that help families set aside money for future college costs.

RESOURCES

Credit Karma. (n.d.). Budgeting for teens: 18 tips for growing your money young. Retrieved from https://www.creditkarma.com/financial-planning/i/budgeting-for-teens

Credit.org. (n.d.). Understanding interest rates: How they work and impact you. Retrieved from https://www.credit.org/blogs/blog-posts/what-are-interest-rates-how-does-interest-work

Desert Financial. (n.d.). Setting SMART financial goals. Retrieved from https://www.desertfinancial.com/en/learn/blog/financial-education/smart-goals

Kids Money. (n.d.). 23 best money apps for teens. Retrieved from https://www.kidsmoney.org/teens/money-management/apps/

Investopedia. (n.d.). How does the envelope budgeting system work? Retrieved from https://www.investopedia.com/envelope-budgeting-system-5208026

Garaus, M., Wagner, U., & Kummer, C. (2021). Factors affecting impulse buying behavior of consumers. *PMC, 10*. Retrieved from https://www.ncbi.nlm.nih.gov/pmc/articles/PMC8206473/

Ramsey Solutions. (n.d.). How to teach teenagers about money. Retrieved from https://www.ramseysolutions.com/relationships/teach-teenagers-about-money

Indeed. (n.d.). Resume examples for teens: Template and writing tips. Retrieved from https://www.indeed.com/career-advice/resumes-cover-letters/resume-examples-for-teens

Oxford Royale. (n.d.). 14 teen entrepreneurs and how they succeeded. Retrieved from https://www.oxford-royale.com/articles/14-teen-entrepreneurs/

goHenry. (n.d.). 24 ways teens can make money online. Retrieved from https://www.gohenry.com/us/blog/financial-education/24-ways-teens-can-make-money-online

Investopedia. (n.d.). Teens and income taxes: Do they need to file? Retrieved from https://www.investopedia.com/teens-and-income-taxes-7152618

Experian. (n.d.). 8 ways to help your teen build good credit now. Retrieved from https://www.experian.com/blogs/ask-experian/how-to-help-your-teen-build-credit/

FDIC. (2023). Credit cards for young adults. Retrieved from https://www.fdic.gov/resources/consumers/consumer-news/2023-08.html

Experian. (n.d.). Good debt vs. bad debt: What's the difference? Retrieved from https://www.experian.com/blogs/ask-experian/good-debt-vs-bad-debt-whats-the-difference/

NerdWallet. (n.d.). Pay off debt: Tools and tips. Retrieved from https://www.nerdwallet.com/article/finance/pay-off-debt

First Alliance Credit Union. (n.d.). How to help teens harness the power of compound interest. Retrieved from https://www.firstalliancecu.com/blog/teach-teens-compound-interest

The Motley Fool. (n.d.). How to start investing as a teenager. Retrieved from https://www.fool.com/investing/how-to-invest/investing-for-teens/

Investopedia. (n.d.). Can teenagers invest in Roth IRAs? Retrieved from https://www.investopedia.com/can-teenagers-invest-in-roth-iras-4770663

Lake City Bank. (n.d.). Tips for opening your teen's first checking account. Retrieved from https://www.lakecitybank.com/teen-checking-account/

Investopedia. (n.d.). What teens need to know about cryptocurrency. Retrieved from https://www.investopedia.com/what-teens-need-to-know-about-cryptocurrency-7152233

CNBC. (2023). How parents can protect teens from mobile app payment issues. Retrieved from https://www.cnbc.com/2023/05/23/how-parents-can-protect-teens-from-mobile-app-payment-issues.html

Call Federal Credit Union. (n.d.). Online financial security for teens. Retrieved from https://callfederal.org/financial-education/financial-insights/online-security-for-teens/

Forbes Advisor. (n.d.). How to open a 529 account: A step-by-step guide. Retrieved from https://www.forbes.com/advisor/student-loans/how-to-open-a-529-plan/

NerdWallet. (n.d.). Guide for the first-time car buyer. Retrieved from https://www.nerdwallet.com/l/first-time-car-buyer

Scholarships360. (n.d.). The ultimate guide to finding & winning scholarships. Retrieved from https://scholarships360.org/scholarships/ultimate-scholarships-guide/

Under30Experiences. (n.d.). Travel hacking: Saving money and finding cheap flights. Retrieved from https://www.under30experiences.com/blog/travel-hacking-saving-money-and-finding-cheap-flights

Harvard Business Review. (2022). How to negotiate your starting salary. Retrieved from https://hbr.org/2022/07/how-to-negotiate-your-starting-salary

New Silver. (n.d.). 3 highly motivational real estate success stories. Retrieved from https://newsilver.com/the-lender/real-estate-success-stories/

Forbes Advisor. (2024). Best budgeting apps of June 2024. Retrieved from https://www.forbes.com/advisor/banking/best-budgeting-apps/

Investopedia. (n.d.). Financial independence, retire early (FIRE) explained. Retrieved from https://www.investopedia.com/terms/f/financial-independence-retire-early-fire.asp